Cavachons

The Owner's Guide from Puppy to Old Age

Choosing, Caring for, Grooming, Health, Training and Understanding Your Cavachon Dog or Puppy

By Morgan Andrews

Copyright and Trademarks

Disclaimer and Legal Notice

Foreword

If you are looking for a friendly, playful, and people-loving dog breed that is great with kids, you need look no further than the Cavachon. This is a crossbreed dog, also sometimes referred to as a 'designer' dog. The breed was developed by crossing a purebred Cavalier King Charles Spaniel with a Bichon Frise, so it exhibits a combination of physical and personality traits from both breeds.

You've made a wise choice in purchasing this book, as many of the world's top Cavachon breeders have been involved in its creation. By the time you have finished, I am certain that you will have all the information required to make that all-important decision on whether the Cavachon is the right breed for you.

My job as an expert trainer and professional dog whisperer is to help you better understand your Cavachon and eliminate behavioral problems before they get out of hand.

Yes, this is an exceptional and wonderful breed with unique and endearing qualities, however it is vitally important that you understand what makes these dogs different and what they will need from you in care and companionship before you proceed. That is the purpose of this book. No matter how cute Cavachons are, they must only go to owners who can understand and take responsibility for the breed's emotional as well as physical needs.

Being responsible in truly considering the ramifications of any pet ownership is a huge part of being a good owner. If you don't do the hard thinking first, before the fun starts, the dog is the one who will face the consequences of your bad choice. However, if you choose wisely and well, taking into consideration your needs and those of the Cavachon, you will have one of the best canine companions you could ever hope to meet.

Certainly I believe that if you learn everything you can about Cavachons, take a realistic look at your life and home, and decide this is the breed for you, you will never regret the decision.

Acknowledgments

In writing this book, I also sought tips, advice, photos, and opinions from many experts on the Cavachon breed. In particular, I wish to thank the following wonderful breeders, organizations, owners, and vets for their outstanding help and contribution:

United States and Canada Contributors

Melanie McCarthy of Cavachons From The Monarchy
http://www.cavachonsfromthemonarchy.com

Linda & Steve Rogers of Timshell Farm
http://www.timshellfarm.com

Linda Kaiser of Smooch My Pups
http://www.smoochmypups.com/

Barby Wolfish of Pet Pointe
http://www.petpointe.ca/

Kenneth Lang of Multiply Cavachons
https://www.facebook.com/groups/cavachon/

Keely Wilkins of Ballyhara
http://www.ballyhara.net

United Kingdom Contributors

Jenna Lovatt of Pawfect Cavachons
http://pawfectcavachons.wixsite.com/pawfectcavachons

Victoria Johnson of Cosmic Cavachons & Cavapoos
http://www.cosmiccavachons.co.uk

Nichola Lack of Cracking Cavachons
http://www.cavachons.co.uk/

Celia M Evans of Scarletstrue
http://www.scarletstrue.com/

Emma Nishigaki of Utsukushi Kennel

Owners:

Sue Tomlin, Robert Maxwell, Katie Maggs, Jen Sweetman, Natalie Mayatt, Lynn Millar, Jan Stocks, Corey Seeman, Liz Priebe and Pat Kelleher.

Photo Credit: Jenna Lovatt of Pawfect Cavachons.

Table of Contents

Table of Contents

Table of Contents

Table of Contents

Table of Contents

Chapter 1 – Meet the Cavachon

I'm assuming you have just gone out and bought your new Cavachon puppy, but if you are still in two minds about whether to get one, or perhaps another breed, don't worry — we are here to guide you with expert breeder advice along the way so you really get to know the Cavachon in order to make the decision.

Experienced breeders from all over the world have kindly given their time to answer questions and give their expert advice. You are about to benefit from literally hundreds of years' experience of breeding and living with Cavachons.

Photo Credit: Victoria Johnson of Cosmic Cavachons & Cavapoos.

Here are some of the reasons **Melanie McCarthy of Cavachons From The Monarchy** believes the Cavachon is so special: "These loving and gentle creatures maintain their 'puppy playfulness' and 'teddy bear' looks into adulthood. In addition, families also report that they are exceptional with children, make wonderful therapy dogs, and do not bark unless it is for a good reason.

"Today, it seems that there is a high percentage of children, and of course, adults, with allergies, some severe. Reports back from families indicate that Cavachons are indeed hypo-allergenic and because of that, many children who otherwise would not be able to own a pet are able to stay healthy with their Cavachons, unlike their experience with most other breeds!

"Having said that, it is worth saying that there is no guarantee that every dog lover with allergies or other health problems will be able to enjoy this feature of a Cavachon and they may still become ill in the presence of a dog. We always require families who report allergies to us ahead of time, to visit us and handle Cavachon puppies in order to see how well they do. Unfortunately there are people who will never be able to be around any type of dog because of allergies or other reaction problems."

Photo Credit: Linda & Steve Rogers of Timshell Farm.

Linda & Steve Rogers of Timshell Farm list some of the best things about the Cavachon breed:

- Sparkly, happy disposition
- Gentler energy/activity level (playful and fun but never hyper or yappy)
- Lower-to-no-shedding coats
- Loyal, loving natures – real 'people' dogs
- BEAUTIFUL faces – 'Teddy Bear' faces: which is a wide face; shorter nose that is more square-shaped, not long or pointy; large, round eyes that are wide spaced, longer ears with

little curls
- Athletic, agile little dogs that love to hike, swim, go for walks, fetch, play...
- High trainability that comes from being intelligent and very eager to please
- Hybrid vigor that minimizes the risk of genetic faults by breeding two distinct purebreds (cleared of genetic faults, of course, prior to breeding)

Crossbreeding dogs is by no means a recent practice – humans have developed hundreds of different dog breeds through selective breeding. Accidental breeding is also fairly common and it sometimes results in crossbreeding. This being the case, it is possible that the first Cavachon was born many years ago but the purposeful crossing of the Cavalier King Charles Spaniel to a Bichon Frise is fairly new, starting in the mid 1990s.

Keely Wilkins of Ballyhara says: "I have been asked so many times what makes a Cavachon special. I have been raising them for over 15 years, and in that time period I have come to know these little dogs intimately as the sweetest, most amiable, easy to deal with and exuberant happy puppies/dogs that I have ever known. They are not hyper, but have a joyful spirit and a zest for life. Their love knows no bounds as they are always eager to please you. They excel at being therapy dogs and really enjoy their job. They have such a kind heart that they really help people and children who have emotional issues.

"With two incredibly amazing dogs put together, you get one fantastic combination of both parents. They are incredibly smart and in my opinion fairly easy to train as long as you're consistent; of course it is very important to start with high-quality parents and to do your research and make sure that the breeder has their dogs health checked and tested for genetic issues."

Linda & Steve Rogers of Timshell Farm: "Cavachons became very popular around 2001.... and of course, there are some breeders that do an exceedingly good job and those who do not. This is a terrible thing for adoptive families, especially those who don't do a lot of research and fall in love with a cute puppy, buy it, and then find out they are in terrible trouble because they didn't research the breeds, didn't find out about the particular genetic faults that follow each purebred, and didn't know that a cute puppy could turn into a CUJO-CHON because the parents had terrible temperaments or mental disorders.

"It is important to note that having good traits in a puppy is no accident. They must be carefully bred in or infused into the mix, by having only the very best parent dogs, tested and **cleared for genetic faults** and also temperament-verified. A breeder should never use a parent dog with any 'issues' whatsoever (nippy, shy/fearful, aggressive/too assertive, hyper, yappy, overactive....) as these traits can come through to the puppy, just like genetic health faults."

Popularity Compared to Other Crossbreeds

The designer dog trend has been sweeping the nation in recent years with crossbreeds like the Labradoodle and the Cavachon gaining a serious following. The term '**designer dog**' is somewhat misleading because the term 'designer' is usually applied to items that are expensive, made by a famous or prestigious designer. In reality, designer dogs are just hybrids. In this case, the term 'designer' is more accurately linked to the word 'fashionable'.

Though crossbreed dogs like the Cavachon will likely never be accepted by major dog registration organizations like the American Kennel Club (AKC) and the UK Kennel Club, there are organizations out there specifically for crossbreed dogs:

American Canine Hybrid Club (ACHC)
http://www.achclub.com/

Designer Breed Registry (DBR)
http://www.designerbreedregistry.com/

International Designer Canine Registry (IDCR)
http://designercanineregistry.com/

Does It Matter That Cavachons Are a Crossbreed?

Without getting into the 'politics' of hybrid dogs, the main thing you should know is that not everyone believes in the benefits of crossbreeds. While it's important to thoroughly research any dog before you adopt, don't let other people's opinions and biases affect your decision.

There are some breeders who feel that crossbreeds are a 'scam', as they sometimes cost more than purebreds without the selectively bred traits. These breeders also don't believe that crossbreeds are healthier than purebreds. Even so, many people find that crossbreeds have more 'vigor' than purebreds and are also less likely to show extreme behaviors.

The theory is that the inbreeding amongst the same gene pool over hundreds of years has bred into pure breeds a multitude of diseases, cancers and bone ailments. **Heterosis**, or **hybrid vigor**, is a scientific theory that when cross breeding two purebred dogs, only

the superior genes carry forward, thus producing a significantly smarter and healthier dog. Some, however, don't believe this to be true, so the issue is controversial in the dog breed world!

Photo Credit: Keely Wilkins of Ballyhara.

It's vital to understand the possible traits and characteristics of a puppy before you buy. While a Cavachon is ideally bred for the Bichon Frise **intelligence and low-shedding coat** and the Cavalier's **friendly attitude**, there is no guarantee that these traits will be passed on. It's equally likely that a puppy will receive the undesirable traits of both parent breeds. The genetic characteristics of a crossbreed are essentially a random mix between the two parents.

The appearance of a Cavachon can also vary. Some mature to look like one of the parents rather than a mixture of both. The size of the breed can also differ. It's common for a hybrid dog to be adopted because of its cute appearance, only to grow up to look completely different.

According to online search statistics gathered by DogTime.com, the top ten most popular hybrid dogs are:

- **Cockapoo** – Cocker Spaniel and Poodle
- **Maltipoo** – Maltese and Poodle
- **Labradoodle** – Labrador Retriever and Poodle
- **Goldendoodle** – Golden Retriever and Poodle
- **Maltese Shih Tzu** – Maltese and Shih Tzu
- **Puggle** – Pug and Beagle
- **Schnoodle** – Schnauzer and Poodle
- **Peekapoo** – Pekingese and Poodle
- **Yorkipoo** – Yorkshire Terrier and Miniature Poodle
- **Goldador** – Golden Retriever and Labrador Retriever

Based on this list, the Cavachon is not one of the top ten most popular crossbreed dogs in the United States. The fact that it is still a fairly new breed may be part of the reason. It may also have something to do with the fact that Poodles and Labrador Retrievers are consistently ranked within the top ten most popular dog breeds (according to AKC registration statistics). Because these breeds are so popular, crossbreeds of these breeds are more common.

Breeding Cavachons – F1, F2, etc.

Crossing a purebred Bichon Frise with a purebred Cavalier King Charles Spaniel will result in a litter of puppies having a 50/50 mix of Bichon Frise and Cavalier King Charles Spaniel blood.

If you breed two Cavachons, or a Cavachon with a purebred Bichon Frise or Cavalier King Charles Spaniel, the ratio will be different. When it comes to breeding hybrid dogs, there is a definite structure and each type of breeding has its own name.

- **F1** – A first generation hybrid is known as an F1 – this is a direct result of breeding two purebred dogs of different breeds. For example, a Cavachon resulting from mating a purebred Bichon Frise and a purebred Cavalier King Charles Spaniel would be an F1.

- **F2** – A second generation hybrid is known as an F2 – this is the result of breeding two F1 dogs together. For example, a Cavachon resulting from breeding two first-generation (F1) Cavachons would be an F2.

- **F3** – A third generation hybrid is known as an F3 – this is the result of breeding two F2 dogs together. For example, a Cavachon resulting from breeding two second-generation (F2) Cavachons would be an F3.

The list goes on and on with each subsequent generation being labeled with the next number. In addition to the crossings described above, hybrid dogs can also be 'backcrossed'. That is, a first-generation hybrid can be bred back to a purebred dog of either parent breed. For example, an F1 Cavachon bred with a purebred Bichon Frise or Cavalier King Charles Spaniel would produce backcrossed puppies – these puppies would be labeled F1b. To produce F2b puppies you would breed an F1 Cavachon to an F1b backcrossed Cavachon.

Emma Nishigaki of Utsukushi Kennel has extensively researched the genetics of the Cavachon and is an expert on this topic. She has some important advice: "It is essential that Cavachons are only produced in F1 form i.e. a Cavachon should never be bred from due to the autosomal recessive conditions of the Cavalier.

"You MUST NOT have a Cavalier gene on both sides even if both parents are tested healthy. The Cavachon should never become a pedigree breed; to do so would involve reintroducing all the complex diseases that a Cavalier can suffer from."

Jen Sweetman, owner of Bailey: "My first piece of advice when buying a Cavachon would be to research the health conditions that puppies can inherit from either parent, mostly the Cavalier King Charles Spaniel. I cannot stress enough how important this is, it really is paramount. Buyers should thoroughly research all genetic conditions and ensure both parents of puppies have been tested and are clear of these awful conditions. I feel so strongly about this that I wouldn't have a puppy from non-health tested parents!"

Cavachon Personality and Temperament

So what defines your Cavachon's character? One factor is his **temperament**, which is an inherited trait, and another factor is the **environment** in which your Cavachon grows up. In a dog's life, the first few months are deemed really important. When the time comes that he becomes separated from the litter, his reactions and responses to the world around him are a reflection of how he has learned the essence of socialization.

Photo Credit: Kenneth Lang of Multiply Cavachons.

There is no denying the **benefits** that your Cavachon gets from being introduced early to other dogs and humans, along with different noises and smells. When a dog learns how to feel comfortable in whatever type of surrounding he is in, feelings of fear and anxiety can be eliminated. Otherwise these feelings can cause a dog to display undesirable behavior such as aggression.

Both Cavalier King Charles Spaniels and Bichon Frise dogs are friendly, social, and affectionate, so you can expect the same from a Cavachon. They tend to be active, fun-loving dogs that form strong bonds with their owners. This breed is friendly with other dogs but, depending how much Cavalier King Charles Spaniel it has, the Cavachon may not get along with birds or small household pets.

Victoria Johnson of Cosmic Cavachons & Cavapoos says: "The Cavachon temperament is a combination of the bubbly, mischievous Bichon Frise and the sweet, gentle Cavalier King Charles Spaniel."

Nichola Lack of Cracking Cavachons: "Cavachons are happy little dogs, (they) want nothing more than for you to love them. They enjoy walks and playing and also love being fussed, so great lap dogs."

The Cavachon is a **playful companion** and a fun-loving breed which makes them an excellent choice for families with children.

Because this breed is so social and people-oriented it may not do well if left alone for long periods of time. Cavachons that do not get enough attention have a higher risk for developing problem behaviors and separation anxiety. If you work a full-time job or do not spend a lot of time at home, the Cavachon **may not be the right breed for you.** Having another dog as a companion and playmate for your Cavachon may help, but these dogs generally prefer human company. These dogs are very eager to please which makes them highly trainable.

Linda & Steve Rogers of Timshell Farm agrees: "Cavaliers are not suited to being left alone – it is just part of their being so human-oriented. Bichons can become more nervous and flighty if left alone for long periods. I think Cavaliers become fearful and withdrawn if left alone.

"The Cavachon is definitely a loyal, human-loving crossbreed but should not be left for long periods alone, otherwise behavior issues can develop and then the breeder gets a call from the owner wanting to know why the dog is acting out. If they are with another puppy or dog, I think this can help, but at least three visits during the day would be my minimum. Options include doggy daycare, pet walker, someone coming home at lunch or a neighbor puppy-sitting."

Because the Cavachon is a crossbreed and therefore not recognized by the American Kennel Club (AKC), it **does not have** an official breed standard. However we can look at the parent breeds to give an idea of physical looks and likely temperament.

All About the Cavalier King Charles Spaniel

The Cavalier King Charles Spaniel has a royal-sounding name and it does, in fact, have something of a royal history. This breed is a small Spaniel typically classified as a toy dog by both the American Kennel Club and the UK Kennel Club.

Photo Credit: Victoria Johnson of Cosmic Cavachons & Cavapoos.

The Cavalier King Charles Spaniel remains **one of the most popular** breeds in the UK due to its playful and affectionate personality, and it is growing increasingly popular in the United States. In 2009, the Cavalier King Charles Spaniel barely made it into the top 25 for AKC registration statistics. The breed's popularity has been growing steadily, however, climbing to 18 in 2013.

The Cavalier King Charles Spaniel is said to be of average intelligence and, due to their hunting instincts, they may be a threat to birds and small household pets.

The Cavalier King Charles Spaniel has an undocked tail that hangs nearly to the ground. Though still **classified as a toy breed**, the Cavalier King Charles Spaniel is one of the largest toy breeds and one of the smallest Spaniels. According to the AKC breed standard, this dog should stand between 12 and 13 inches (30 to 33 cm) tall and weigh between 10 and 18 pounds (4.5 to 8.2 kg).

The coat of the Cavalier King Charles Spaniel is long and silky without curl, but some dogs may have slightly wavy coats. Most specimens of the breed exhibit feathering of the fur on the ears, feet, legs, and tail – this feathering is one of the breed's defining features. The breed standard dictates that it be kept long.

The Cavalier King Charles Spaniel comes in **four different colors,** according to the breed standard – Blenheim, tri-color, black-and-tan, and ruby.

The **Blenheim** coloration is the most common and it consists of chestnut white markings (typically on the ears, face, back and legs) over a pearly white background. This coloration is named for Blenheim Palace, the home of John Churchill. Churchill raised the dogs that became the predecessors of the modern Cavalier King Charles Spaniel with this type of coloration.

Dogs with **tri-color** patterning exhibit a black and white coloration with tan markings on the cheeks, ears, eyebrows, inside the legs, and under the tail – this coloration is sometimes referred to as Prince Charles.

The **black-and-tan** coloration consists of a black body with tan highlights on the cheeks, eyebrows, legs, and under the tail.

Ruby Cavalier King Charles Spaniels exhibit chestnut coloration all over the body.

Cavalier King Charles Spaniel History

The exact origins of the Cavalier King Charles Spaniel are unknown, but they are known to have descended from various toy Spaniels that can be seen in 16th, 17th, and 18th century paintings by famous artists like Lely, Gainsborough, Titian, and Van Dyck. The Spaniels in these paintings exhibit several characteristics shown by modern day Cavalier King Charles Spaniels, including a flat head and almond-shaped eyes.

During the reign of King Charles II, toy Spaniels were popular among the wealthier classes. In fact, King Charles II himself was rarely seen without two or three toy Spaniels at his heels. King Charles II even wrote a decree requiring that King Charles Spaniels, as they were called at the time, be allowed in all public areas – even the Houses of Parliament.

During the early years of the King Charles Spaniel there was no recognized breed standard, so the type and size of this breed varied. By the mid-19th century, however, dog breeding and dog showing became more popular, so there developed a need for a breed standard. At the time, toy Spaniels with a flat face, undershot jaw, and domed skull with round eyes and low-set ears became fashionable. As a result, the King Charles Spaniel that was depicted

in early paintings became almost extinct.

In 1926, American breeder Roswell Eldridge sought to revive the breed as depicted in those early paintings; he searched far and wide all across Europe for foundation stock. Because he was only able to find short-faced King Charles Spaniels, he appealed to the Kennel Club and was granted permission to offer prizes at the Crufts Dog Show for Spaniels of the Blenheim variety that looked like the dogs depicted in paintings from King Charles II's time.

Unfortunately, the challenge was not taken seriously by King Charles breeders. It wasn't until 1928 that someone was awarded the prize. The prize went to Ann's Son, a dog owned by Miss Mostyn Walker. During this same year, the Cavalier King Charles Spaniel Club (CKSC) was founded. The club developed the first breed standard for the Cavalier King Charles Spaniel, and the standard remains largely the same to this day.

The Cavalier King Charles Spaniel came to be recognized by the Kennel Club in 1945 and was brought to the United States a few years later. The first US-based breed club was founded in 1954 and the breed was accepted for AKC registration as part of the Miscellaneous class in 1954.

The AKC offered the Cavalier King Charles Spaniel Club the position of 'official breed club' in 1992, but members of the club resisted because they feared that it would result in breeders straying from the breed standard. Several years later, a few members from the CKSC formed a new club, the American Cavalier King Charles Spaniel Club (ACKSC). The club was awarded the status of parent club for the Cavalier King Charles Spaniel and the breed was formally recognized by the AKC in 1995.

Cavalier Health

Unfortunately, the selective breeding of Cavaliers has led to the development of a number of hereditary health problems. These include **Mitral Valve Disease** – a serious condition that can cause death or epilepsy – and a condition affecting the spine called **Syringomyelia**.

These are serious conditions that can cause widespread pain and early death. Mitral Valve Disease, in particular, is of increasing concern amongst Cavalier breeders. It's a disease that affects (in varying degrees of seriousness) about 50% of all purebred Cavaliers by the time they reach ten years old, although MVD can be managed with medication. For this reason, top breeders of Cavaliers should provide proof that a puppy has healthy parents.

The Cavalier's health problems are one of the reasons why the Cavachon is becoming more popular. F1 Cavachons, which are the direct offspring of a Cavalier, are thought to be less likely to suffer from the breed's genetic conditions, although there is still debate about whether hybrid dogs are less likely to suffer from genetic conditions. Whether designer puppies are healthier or not, there is always a chance that a Cavachon will inherit genetic conditions.

The Cavalier Temperament

There are few breeds that can match the unassuming friendliness of the Cavalier King Charles Spaniel. Cavaliers seem to love everybody and always want a stroke or cuddle from strangers. This makes them excellent family pets, but poor guard dogs.

Cavaliers are intelligent dogs that are happy to please, however they do have a 'mind of their own', to which many Cavalier owners will attest! This means they need to be properly trained using positive reinforcement techniques to avoid developing bad behaviors such as ignoring commands.

Many people think that Cavaliers are quiet dogs. This is not always the case. While some Cavaliers won't bark even if an intruder enters the home, others love nothing more than to bark manically at the smallest noise. A parent Cavalier with a barking tendency often passes this trait down to its offspring. If possible, spend some time with the Cavalier parent before adopting a Cavachon to see whether it's prone to barking.

Cavaliers are companion dogs that are happiest when spending time with humans and other dogs. They shouldn't be left in kennels or by themselves for long periods of time and need plenty of attention. The dogs do, however, make great apartment pets, provided they get daily exercise.

All About the Bichon Frise

The Bichon Frise is a very recognizable breed, known for its small size and fluffy white coat. These dogs have a compact body structure with a rounded skull and curled tail. The Bichon Frise typically weighs between 10 and 20 lbs. (5 to 10 kg) at maturity and stands 9 to 12 inches (23 to 30 cm) high at the withers.

These dogs are sometimes mistaken for miniature Poodles because their coats are so similar - in fact the Bichon Frise does share several similarities with the Poodle. The Bichon Frise has dark, round eyes and a black nose with well-furred drop ears.

The coat of this breed is dense and curly but it does not shed much because loose hairs get caught in the coat rather than falling to the ground. This being the case, the Bichon Frise is sometimes referred to as a hypoallergenic breed. This is not completely true, because the dog does shed (although minimally) and it still produces dander. There is technically no such thing as a hypoallergenic dog (unless it has no hair at all), but the Bichon Frise is less likely to cause a problem for allergy sufferers.

Though white is the most common color for Bichon Frise dogs, they also come in apricot or gray.

The Bichon Frise's coat can be cut in several different ways depending on whether the dog is being kept as a pet or trained for show. The Show Cut is the most recognizable option and it involves letting the coat grow long and full, then trimming and shaping it to follow the contours of the dog's body. The Puppy Cut is a shorter style with the hair trimmed close to the body, leaving it longer on the head and tail. The Panda Cut is between the Show Cut and the Puppy Cut – the hair is trimmed and shaped to follow the contours of the dog's body but it is shorter than the Show Cut and longer than the Puppy Cut.

In terms of temperament, the Bichon Frise is a cheerful and merry little dog. These dogs are playful and affectionate with family and they are generally well-mannered around the house. The Bichon Frise is a very social breed that loves to spend time with his owners and he also enjoys meeting new people. These dogs tend to get along well with dogs and other household pets – they are also very good with children.

Training the Bichon Frise is not particularly difficult, especially if you start while the puppy is still young. This breed does not tend to be strong-willed or independent, though a firm and consistent hand in training is always recommended for the best results. For the most part, Bichon Frise dogs do very well with obedience training.

Bichon Frise History

The Bichon Frise belongs to the Non-Sporting Group for the American Kennel Club and to the Toy Dog group for the UK Kennel Club.

The Bichon Frise has a long history, going all the way back to the 1300s when the Queen of France bred her Poodle with her Maltese to produce the first Bichon Frise litter. The Bichon Frise is descended from the Barbet, a French water dog that played a role in the development of many modern breeds, and the Standard Poodle.

The name Bichon Frise comes from the Middle French word *bichon* which means 'small long-haired dog'. There are also those who believe that *bichon* is a shortened version of the word *barbichon* which means 'small poodle'. This is unlikely to be true, however, because the word *bichon* is actually older than the word *barbichon*.

During the early years of the breed there were actually four different types of Bichon dogs – the Bichon Bolognaise, the Bichon Maltese, the Bichon Havanese, and the Bichon Tenerife. All four breed varieties originated in the Mediterranean and were ferried all over the world by sailors. Not only did these dogs serve as merry travel companions, but they were also used by sailors as barter. During the 12th century, these same sailors brought the dog to the island of Tenerife, one of the Canary Islands south of Spain. In the 14th century, the Bichon Tenerife was transported back to Spain by Italian sailors and the breed quickly grew in popularity, particularly among the wealthy.

The Bichon Tenerife made its first appearance in France during the reign of Francis I (1515-1547) and its popularity soared during the reign of Henry III (1574-1589). There is a legend about King Henry's love for his Bichon being so great that he carried the dog with him everywhere he went, in a basket hung around his neck. The King's love for the Bichon breed served to increase the popularity of the breed at court and the pampering these dogs frequently received gave birth to the French verb *bichonner*, or 'to pamper or make beautiful'.

The popularity of the Bichon breed waned during the 19th century to the point where Bichons came to be kept not as royal pets but as street dogs during the late 1800s.

After World War I ended, fanciers of the breed fought to save the breed from dying out. Renewed interest in the Bichon breed is partially credited to the success of Hergé's *The Adventures of Tintin* which feature a small white dog named Milou, which was actually a fox terrier, but its appearance was described in a way that made it similar to the fluffy white-coated Bichon.

In 1933, the Société Centrale Canine, the French national kennel club, adopted an official standard for the breed. At that time the Bichon was still known by two names – the Bichon and the Tenerife. So, when the Fédération Cynologique Interionationale (FCI) accepted the breed in 1934, it proposed a new name based on the breed's characteristics – Bichon Frise, *frisé* meaning 'curly', in reference to the dog's curly coat.

In 1955, the first Bichon Frise was brought to the United States and the first US-born litter was born a year later in 1956. It wasn't until 1971, however, that the Bichon Frise became eligible for AKC registration as part of the Miscellaneous Class. Two years later, in 1973, the breed was moved to the Non-Sporting Group and it remains there today.

The Bichon Frise continues to be a very popular breed in the United States and it even won Best-in-Show at the Westminster Kennel Club Dog Show in 2001. According to AKC registration statistics, the Bichon Frise was the 40th most popular breed in the United States in 2013, although it dropped a little to 43rd place in 2014.

What Does the Cavachon Look Like?

Because the Cavachon is a crossbreed dog, it does not have its own breed standard. The physical characteristics and personality traits of a Cavachon will vary depending on breeding and how much of each parent's bloodline is present. For the most part, however, you can expect a Cavachon to be a small dog which typically stands between 12 and 13 inches (30.5 to 33 cm) tall and weighs between 15 and 18 pounds (6.8 to 8.2 kg). The Cavachon has big beautiful dark eyes.

The coat of a Cavachon is a medium-length curly or wavy coat. In the first six months, the Cavachon's coat is silky and grows long, then at approximately six months their permanent wavy coat comes in.

Coat Colors

Every litter of Cavachons will be a little bit different in terms of physical appearance, based on the appearance of the parent dogs. The Bichon Frise is usually white in color with a medium-length fluffy coat, though peach and gray colorations are possible. The Cavalier King Charles Spaniel comes in four different colors – white with chestnut markings, black with tan markings, tri-color, or solid chestnut.

The coloration of the parent dogs will determine the coloration of the Cavachon. For the most part, however, Cavachons have medium-length wavy coats with colors of **Blenheim** (white with apricot patches), **tri-color** (black, white, and tan or black and white) or **ruby** (dark apricot with little or no white).

We asked **Jenna Lovatt of Pawfect Cavachons** what coat colours are most popular with prospective owners: "Cavachons do fade. A lot of owners go for solid apricot and black and white."

Do Cavachons Get Along with Children?

Because the Cavachon is such a social and people-loving breed, it does very well with children. The Bichon Frise is one of the most even-tempered breeds out there, likely to get along with everyone and everything. The Cavalier King Charles Spaniel is also very good with children and it loves to play.

Photo Credit: Imogen with Belle from Katie Maggs.

As is true for any dog, it is important that you supervise any interaction between your children and the dog. Young children may not understand that a small dog like the Cavachon is fragile and they might unknowingly hurt the dog or treat it too roughly. You are unlikely to have any trouble with your Cavachon interacting with children, but all dogs have the capacity to become aggressive if they are frightened or mistreated. Teach your children how to properly handle a dog, especially when it is still a puppy, to prevent incidents.

Even if you do not have children, it's advisable to expose your dog to children during puppyhood to prepare the animal to behave correctly during any future encounters. Being good around children is a critical part of any well-behaved dog's repertoire of manners.

Don't tolerate rough or aggressive play from either, and explain to children that Cavachons like 'nice touches'. When puppies get too rough or mouth their fingers when teething, respond with a firm, 'No!'. Soon enough, all parties will get the point.

For prospective owners with young children, I'd encourage them to select a puppy from a breeder who has socialized their dogs with children of all ages. This helps to make sure the puppy is confident enough around children to tolerate their odd sounds and movements. Likewise, temperament is key — a shy, reserved, or anxious puppy should never be considered for a home with children. When inviting a puppy to live in a home with children, it is important to have a crate or other safe space for the puppy to retreat to when the kids become too much!

Owner Jen Sweetman says: "Cavachons are so good with children. My son was 3 when we got Bailey, he is now 6, and they are the best of friends. I also feel it has taught my son that animals should be respected, just as humans should, and gives him the opportunity to grow up having a little responsibility and being involved with all aspects of Bailey's general health and wellbeing."

Do Cavachons Get Along with Other Animals?

The Bichon Frise is a friendly breed that will get along with just about anyone or anything. These dogs are great around other dogs and they rarely have problems with household pets like cats.

The Cavalier King Charles Spaniel also does very well around other dogs but as a Spaniel, the Cavalier King Charles Spaniel has a fairly high prey drive, so it might view cats and small household pets (especially birds) as prey and chase them.

For the most part, the Cavachon is excellent with other dogs and you are unlikely to have a problem with other pets. Still, you should supervise early interactions in neutral territory between your Cavachon and other animals until you know how they will behave.

Raising your Cavachon from a puppy in a household with other pets is your best bet for making sure that your dog does well around other animals.

Photo Credit: Bob and Leia from Natalie Mayatt.

Chapter 2 – Cavachon Dog Breed Standard

Since the Cavachon is not an official breed, the following are the official breed standards for the parent breeds. This will give you some idea of the traits and look of the Cavachon based on the two foundation breeds.

The breed standard provides the main blueprint for a number of dog attributes that include a dog breed's physical appearance, his unique moves, and the type of temperament that each breed is expected to have. Created and laid down by the breed societies, dogs that are purebred (pedigree) have their registrations kept by the American Kennel Club and the Kennel Club (in the UK).

http://www.akc.org/
https://www.thekennelclub.org.uk/

Breeders approved by the Kennel Clubs have consented to breed puppies based on strict standards of breeding. They do not just simply mate any available male or female (sire or dam).

These American Kennel Club (AKC) standards are produced verbatim. The only changes incorporated are typographical to enhance readability.

AKC Standard for the Cavalier King Charles Spaniel - Approved Date: January 10, 1995 - Effective Date: April 30, 1995

General Appearance: The Cavalier King Charles Spaniel is an active, graceful, well-balanced toy spaniel, very gay and free in action; fearless and sporting in character, yet at the same time gentle and affectionate. It is this typical gay temperament, combined with true elegance and royal appearance which are of paramount importance in the breed. Natural appearance with no trimming, sculpting or artificial alteration is essential to breed type.

Size - Height 12 to 13 inches at the withers; weight proportionate to height, between 13 and 18 pounds. A small, well balanced dog within these weights is desirable, but these are ideal heights and weights and slight variations are permissible.

Proportion - The body approaches squareness, yet if measured from point of shoulder to point of buttock, is slightly longer than the height at the withers. The height from the withers to the elbow is approximately equal to the height from the elbow to the ground.

Substance - Bone moderate in proportion to size. Weedy and coarse specimens are to be equally penalized.

Head - Proportionate to size of dog, appearing neither too large nor too small for the body.

Expression - The sweet, gentle, melting expression is an important breed characteristic.

Photo Credit: Victoria Johnson of Cosmic Cavachons & Cavapoos.

Eyes - Large, round, but not prominent and set well apart; color a warm, very dark brown; giving a lustrous, limpid look. Rims dark. There should be cushioning under the eyes which contributes to the soft expression. Faults - small, almond-shaped, prominent, or light eyes; white surrounding ring.

Ears - Set high, but not close, on top of the head. Leather long with plenty of feathering and wide enough so that when the dog is alert, the ears fan slightly forward to frame the face.

Skull - Slightly rounded, but without dome or peak; it should appear flat because of the high placement of the ears. Stop is moderate, neither filled nor deep.

Muzzle - Full muzzle slightly tapered. Length from base of stop to tip of nose about 1½ inches. Face well filled below eyes. Any tendency towards snippiness undesirable. Nose pigment uniformly black without flesh marks and nostrils well developed. Lips well developed but not pendulous giving a clean finish. Faults - Sharp or pointed muzzles.

Bite - A perfect, regular and complete scissors bite is preferred, i.e. the upper teeth closely overlapping the lower teeth and set square into the jaws. Faults - undershot bite, weak or crooked teeth, crooked jaws.

Neck - Fairly long, without throatiness, well enough muscled to form a slight arch at the crest. Set smoothly into nicely sloping shoulders to give an elegant look.

Topline - Level both when moving and standing.

Body - Short-coupled with ribs well sprung but not barreled. Chest moderately deep, extending to elbows allowing ample heart room. Slightly less body at the flank than at the last rib, but with no tucked-up appearance.

Tail - Well set on, carried happily but never much above the level of the back, and in constant characteristic motion when the dog is in action. Docking is optional. If docked, no more than one third to be removed.

Forequarters: Shoulders well laid back. Forelegs straight and well under the dog with elbows close to the sides. Pasterns strong and feet compact with well-cushioned pads. Dewclaws may be removed.

Hindquarters: The hindquarters construction should come down from a good broad pelvis, moderately muscled; stifles well turned and hocks well let down. The hindlegs when viewed from the rear should parallel each other from hock to heel. Faults - Cow or sickle hocks.

Coat: Of moderate length, silky, free from curl. Slight wave permissible. Feathering on ears, chest, legs and tail should be long, and the feathering on the feet is a feature of the breed. No trimming of the dog is permitted. Specimens where the coat has been altered by trimming, clipping, or by artificial means shall be so severely penalized as to be effectively eliminated from competition. Hair growing between the pads on the underside of the feet may be trimmed.

Color: <u>Blenheim</u> - Rich chestnut markings well broken up on a clear, pearly white ground. The ears must be chestnut and the color evenly spaced on the head and surrounding both eyes, with a white blaze between the eyes and ears, in the center of which may be the lozenge or 'Blenheim spot'. The lozenge is a unique and desirable, though not essential, characteristic of the Blenheim.

<u>Tricolor</u> - Jet black markings well broken up on a clear, pearly white ground. The ears must be black and the color evenly spaced on the head and surrounding both eyes, with a white blaze between the eyes. Rich tan markings over the eyes, on cheeks, inside ears and on underside of tail.

<u>Ruby</u> - Whole-colored rich red.

<u>Black and Tan</u> - Jet black with rich, bright tan markings over eyes, on cheeks, inside ears, on chest, legs, and on underside of tail.

Faults - Heavy ticking on Blenheims or Tricolors, white marks on Rubies or Black and Tans.

Gait - Free moving and elegant in action, with good reach in front and sound, driving rear action. When viewed from the side, the movement exhibits a good length of stride, and viewed from front and rear it is straight and true, resulting from straight-boned fronts and properly made and muscled hindquarters.

Temperament - Gay, friendly, non-aggressive with no tendency towards nervousness or shyness. Bad temper, shyness, and meanness are not to be tolerated and are to be severely penalized as to effectively remove the specimen from competition.

AKC Standard for the Bichon Frise - Approved October 11, 1988 Effective November 30, 1988

General Appearance: The Bichon Frise is a small, sturdy, white powder puff of a dog whose merry temperament is evidenced by his plumed tail carried jauntily over the back and his darkeyed inquisitive expression. This is a breed that has no gross or incapacitating exaggerations and therefore there is no inherent reason for lack of balance or unsound movement. Any deviation from the ideal described in the standard should be penalized to the extent of the deviation. Structural faults common to all breeds are as undesirable in the Bichon Frise as in any other breed, even though such faults may not be specifically mentioned in the standard.

Size - Dogs and bitches 9½ to 11½ inches are to be given primary preference. Only where the comparative superiority of a specimen outside this range clearly justifies it should greater latitude be taken. In no case, however, should this latitude ever extend over 12 inches or under 9 inches. The minimum limits do not apply to puppies.

Proportion - The body from the forward-most point of the chest to the point of rump is one-quarter longer than the height at the withers. The body from the withers to lowest point of chest represents half the distance from withers to ground.

Substance - Compact and of medium bone throughout; neither coarse nor fine.

Head: Expression - Soft, dark-eyed, inquisitive, alert.

Eyes are round, black or dark brown and are set in the skull to look directly forward. An overly large or bulging eye is a fault as is an almond shaped, obliquely set eye. Halos, the black or very dark brown skin surrounding the eyes, are necessary as they accentuate the eye and enhance expression. The eye rims themselves must be black. Broken pigment, or total absence of pigment on the eye rims produce a blank and staring expression, which is a definite fault. Eyes of any color other than black or dark brown are a very serious fault and must be severely penalized.

Ears are drop and are covered with long flowing hair. When extended toward the nose, the leathers reach approximately halfway the length of the muzzle. They are set on slightly higher than eye level and rather forward on the skull, so that when the dog is alert they serve to frame the face. The **skull** is slightly rounded, allowing for a round and forward looking eye. The stop is slightly accentuated.

Muzzle - A properly balanced head is three parts muzzle to five parts skull, measured from the nose to the stop and from the stop to the occiput. A line drawn between the outside corners of the eyes and to the nose will create a near equilateral triangle. There is a slight degree of chiseling under the eyes, but not so much as to result in a weak or snipey foreface. The lower jaw is strong. The nose is prominent and always black. Lips are black, fine, never drooping. **Bite** is scissors. A bite which is undershot or overshot should be severely penalized. A crooked or out of line tooth is permissible, however, missing teeth are to be severely faulted.

Neck, Topline and Body: The arched **neck** is long and carried proudly behind an erect head. It blends smoothly into the shoulders. The length of neck from occiput to withers is approximately one-third the distance from forechest to buttocks.

The **topline** is level except for a slight, muscular arch over the loin. **Body** - The chest is well developed and wide enough to allow free and unrestricted movement of the front legs. The lowest point of the chest extends at least to the elbow. The rib cage is moderately sprung and extends back to a short and muscular loin. The forechest is well pronounced and protrudes slightly forward of the point of shoulder. The underline has a moderate tuck-up. **Tail** is well plumed, set on level with the topline and curved gracefully over the back so that the hair of the tail rests on the back. When the tail is extended toward the head it reaches at least halfway to the withers. A low tail set, a tail carried perpendicularly to the back, or a tail which droops behind is to be severely penalized. A corkscrew tail is a very serious fault.

Forequarters: Shoulders - The shoulder blade, upper arm and forearm are approximately equal in length. The shoulders are laid back to somewhat near a forty-five degree angle. The upper arm extends well back so the elbow is placed directly below the withers when viewed from the side. Legs are of medium bone; straight, with no bow or curve in the forearm or wrist. The elbows are held close to the body. The pasterns slope slightly from the vertical. The dewclaws may be removed. The feet are tight and round, resembling those of a cat and point directly forward, turning neither in nor out. Pads are black. Nails are kept short.

Hindquarters: The hindquarters are of medium bone, well angulated with muscular thighs and spaced moderately wide. The upper and lower thigh are nearly equal in length, meeting at a well bent stifle joint. The leg from hock joint to foot pad is perpendicular to the ground. Dewclaws may be removed. Paws are tight and round with black pads.

Coat: The texture of the coat is of utmost importance. The undercoat is soft and dense, the outercoat of a coarser and curlier texture. The combination of the two gives a soft but substantial feel to the touch which is similar to plush or velvet and when patted springs back. When bathed and brushed, it stands off the body, creating an overall powder puff appearance. A wiry coat is not desirable. A limp, silky coat, a coat that lies down, or a lack of undercoat are very serious faults. **Trimming** - The coat is trimmed to reveal the natural outline of the body. It is rounded off from any direction and never cut so short as to create an overly trimmed or squared off appearance. The furnishings of the head, beard, moustache, ears and tail are left longer. The longer head hair is trimmed to create an overall rounded impression. The topline is trimmed to appear level. The coat is long enough to maintain the powder puff look which is characteristic of the breed.

Color: Color is white, may have shadings of buff, cream or apricot around the ears or on the body. Any color in excess of 10 percent of the entire coat of a mature specimen is a fault and should be penalized, but color of the accepted shadings should not be faulted in puppies.

Gait: Movement at a trot is free, precise and effortless. In profile the forelegs and hind legs extend equally with an easy reach and drive that maintain a steady topline. When moving, the head and neck remain somewhat erect and as speed increases there is a very slight convergence of legs toward the center line. Moving away, the

hindquarters travel with moderate width between them and the foot pads can be seen. Coming and going, his movement is precise and true.

Photo Credit: from Melanie McCarthy of Cavachons From The Monarchy

Temperament: Gentle mannered, sensitive, playful and affectionate. A cheerful attitude is the hallmark of the breed and one should settle for nothing less.

Chapter 3 – Is a Cavachon the Right Dog for You?

When you have moved past the stage of just 'window shopping' for a dog and think you're pretty well settled on a Cavachon, there are questions you need to ask, and some basic education to acquire.

Cavachon 'people' need to be patient, loving, flexible dog owners who are committed to training their pets and creating an environment for them that supports their wellbeing, their best behavior, and gives them emotional security.

Photo Credit: Linda & Steve Rogers of Timshell Farm.

You also must understand that you could be signing on for a 10-15 year (or more) relationship with an intelligent and fairly demanding little dog. Understand from the beginning that your Cavachon will not settle down and become an adult emotionally for 12-18 months. Many owners give up on their Cavachons during this crucial period of life, choosing instead to give the dogs away or to abandon them at shelters. If any of this sounds like more than you can handle, then re-evaluate your desire to own a Cavachon!

Think about what's going on in your own life. Don't purchase a dog at a time when you have a huge commitment at work or there's a lot of disruption around an impending holiday. Dogs, especially **very smart ones** like Cavachons, thrive on routine. You want adequate time to bond with your pet, and to help the little dog understand how his new world 'runs'.

We asked some of our contributing breeders some questions to help you decide if the Cavachon is the right dog for you.

Is the Cavachon suitable for a person or family that works all day?

Jenna Lovatt of Pawfect Cavachons: "Cavachons are companion dogs, therefore they require a considerable amount of affection. It's advisable that prospective owners do not leave them alone all day. Working families can consider their needs and arrange dog walkers or doggy day care."

Is the Cavachon breed suitable for a first-time dog owner?

Celia M Evans of Scarletstrue believes so: "Yes, the Cavachon F1 is very much so suitable for a first time dog owner, the Cavachon F1 is a very easy social dog which is suitable for all ages and genders."

Some owners seek a breed suitable for barking and offering a guard dog role – how does the Cavachon match up to that role?

Jenna Lovatt of Pawfect Cavachons: "Cavachons are not a breed considered to be guard dogs, although they are very intelligent and can alert you if someone is entering your garden or at your door."

Some breeds can be described as greedy and prone to weight issues. Would this apply to the Cavachon?

Jenna Lovatt of Pawfect Cavachons says: "Cavachons are not greedy. They enjoy their meals but know their limits. They do not suffer with weight issues."

Do I Need a License?

Before you consider buying your Cavachon, you need to think about whether there are any licensing restrictions in your area. Some countries have strict licensing requirements for the keeping of particular animals.

Even if you are not legally required to have a license for your Cavachon, you might still want to consider getting one. Having a license for your dog means that there is an official record of your ownership so, should someone find your dog when he gets lost, that person will be able to find your contact information and reconnect you with him.

Although there are no federal regulations in the United States regarding the licensing of dogs, most states do require that dogs be licensed by their owners, otherwise you may be subject to a fine. Fortunately, dog licenses are inexpensive (usually around $25) and fairly easy to obtain – you simply file an application with the state and then renew the license each year.

Positives and Negatives of Owning a Cavachon

Every breed of dog has its own list of advantages and disadvantages. If you are thinking about buying a Cavachon you would do well to consider both, although it's a very subjective business since what one person may love in a breed another person will not like at all.

People who love Cavachons should be ready to talk about their good qualities as well as the challenges they pose for one overriding reason – a desire to see these very special animals go to the best home possible where they will be loved and appreciated. I would rather 'put someone off' than see a Cavachon bought and then slowly neglected over time by a less-than-committed owner.

Pros of Cavachon Ownership

- Cavachons remain fairly small, which makes them suitable for apartment or condo life.
- Very friendly and loving breed – they make a great family pet.
- Social, so they get along well with other dogs and most pets.
- Generally fairly easy to breed, not prone to dominance or

willfulness.

- Low-shedding breed, though regular brushing is still recommended.
- The Cavachon is a very healthy breed for the most part, presuming careful breeding.

Possible Negatives of Cavachon Ownership

- The Cavachon is a fairly high-maintenance breed in terms of the amount of attention it needs.
- Love everyone they meet so they do not make good watchdogs or guard dogs.
- Requires professional grooming on average every 5 weeks.
- Cavachons that don't get enough attention may develop problem behaviors.

Owner Jen Sweetman has no regrets: "They are so loving with such a gentle nature, love to be near you and make the best family pet. They can be very mischievous, but that's part of the fun of owning one! If you're happy, they're happy in my experience. They just go with the flow of your day to day life and follow your routine quite happily."

Owner Sue Tomlin says: "My experience of buying a health-tested puppy was an extremely pleasurable one. I encountered no issues whatsoever. I did my research, found my breeder, and from then on it was amazing. I waited a good few months, but held out for a good breeder and a health-tested puppy. I have seen scan photos, birthing videos, many videos from the Facebook page and many were live videos. Lots of updates with photos and messages about worming and weights. It truly was the best experience. In Elsie I have a confident, bold, well socialised puppy. I have had no issues regarding her health or her behaviour. She settled in marvellously from day 1. When I first searched I was looking on main pet selling websites and soon found out that wasn't the route for me. I learnt about F1, F1b, and F2 Cavachons, injections and worming, over-vaccinating and trying for natural methods. Our breeder offers a lifetime support which is invaluable. Overall the experience was nothing short of amazing, the process went without a hitch, but the best thing for me was being so involved at the start and all the way through."

The Cavachon Puppy

Bringing a new puppy home is fun, even if the memories you're making include epic, puppy-generated messes! Young Cavachons are a huge responsibility no matter how much you love them, and they take a lot of work. Cavachon pups are **curious** and they often will have short, chaotic bursts of energy for around 10 minutes until they calm down again!

Photo Credit: Melanie McCarthy of Cavachons From The Monarchy.

The first few weeks with any dog **is an important phase** that shapes the animal's adult behavior and temperament. Every new pet owner hopes to have a well-mannered, obedient, and happy companion.

Puppy proofing, house training, grooming, and feeding aren't the only requirements. Critical socialization must also occur, including crate training. These measures prevent problem behaviors like whining, biting, or jumping.

To achieve these goals, **you must understand** the breed with which you're working. You will need to train him to understand that you are above him in the pecking order and teach him some basic house rules, and you will be rewarded with a companion for life.

If you don't have the time to spend working with your Cavachon in the areas that will make him a desirable companion, ask yourself if this is really the time in your life to have a pet.

Also, bear in mind that you are also your Cavachon's companion. This is not a one-sided relationship. What is your work schedule? Do you have to travel often and for extended periods? Only purchase a Cavachon if you have time to spend with him.

Initially you will need to devote several hours a day to your new puppy. You have to housetrain and feed him every day, giving him your attention and starting to slowly introduce the house rules as well as take care of his general health and welfare. Remember, too, that treating Cavachons like babies is something many owners succumb to and this is not at all good for them.

Certainly for the first few days one of your family **should be around** at all times of the day to help him settle and to start bonding with him. The last thing you should do is buy a puppy and leave him alone in the house after just a day or two. Left alone all day, they will feel isolated, bored, and sad, and this leads to behavioral problems.

Melanie McCarthy of Cavachons From The Monarchy: "We do not sell to families where both partners work full-time and are going to leave the puppy in during the day. What is the point of having a puppy if both are working? An older dog may be more appropriate.

"A 10 week old pup cannot be left alone except for a lunch 'walk' with an outside walker. This puppy will certainly develop separation anxiety. Cavachons, especially since they are bred for companionship, cannot be left alone for more than 2-3 hours once a day until they are more mature, maybe 6 months of age and even then, they should go to puppy day care, not be left alone all day except for a midday walk.

"Someone should be at home full time for at least 4 weeks of potty training; if the partners cannot do it, maybe they have a nanny, or relatives that will step in; otherwise they are not ready for a new puppy.

"Even after 4 weeks of training, the puppy will need to be taken out every 1.5–2 hours all day long. The last potty time would be about

10 p.m. and then at wake up about 5:30 a.m. By 4 weeks of training, the pup will sleep through the night - if and only if they are taken out every approx 2 hours during the day, then played with and fully exercised, to expend their puppy energy all day long.

"Cavachon puppies need intimate companionship on a daily basis; the few times we had complaints about puppy behavior were, regrettably, from owners who took off one week to be with their puppies, then left them for hours on end while they worked. The tension that that creates leads to problem behaviors. There is no doubt in my mind."

DID YOU KNOW? Research shows many dogs have intelligence and understanding levels similar to a two-year-old child. They can understand around 150 words and can solve problems as well as devise tricks to play on people and other animals.

Puppy or Adult?

After you decide that you want a Cavachon, you still have an important decision to make – do you want to purchase a puppy or an adult dog? There are pros and cons to each side of the issue so you should think carefully before you make your decision.

People love puppies for all the obvious reasons. They are adorable, and the younger the dog when you buy him, the longer your time with your pet. At an average **lifespan prediction of 10-15 years**, Cavachons are long-lived in relation to their size.

When you purchase a Cavachon puppy you get to raise the puppy in whatever way you like – you have the power to influence his temperament through socialization and you can also train him as you like. A downside to puppies is that their personalities may change as they grow and develop – picking a puppy based on personality may backfire on you because the adult dog could be very different from the puppy.

While raising a Cavachon puppy can be fun and exciting, it is also very challenging. If you purchase a puppy you will have to deal with things like teething, potty training, and obedience training. Puppies tend to get into mischief so you might have to deal with problem behaviors like chewing or whining.

Buying or adopting an adult Cavachon will not necessarily spare you from all of these challenges, but the dog will probably already be housebroken and might have some training under its belt.

When you do take in a rescue dog, find out as much as possible about the dog's background and the reason for its surrender. Cavachons are often given up for issues with digging, barking, and aggression toward other dogs. If these problems are a consequence of environment or treatment, however, it may be possible to correct them. Additionally, pets living with the elderly are frequently surrendered when their owner dies or goes into a care facility. The animals are homeless, but perfectly well-behaved.

Adopting an adult dog is a good idea for a number of other reasons as well. There are millions of homeless pets living in animal shelters around the country, so adopting an adult dog rather than buying a puppy will help to reduce the unwanted pet population. In adopting a Cavachon you could also be saving the dog's life – most shelters do not euthanize pets anymore but some still do.

A word of warning however - while Cavachons are loveable additions to families they are not our children! We disrespect them by not allowing them to fully be the creatures they were intended to be. Dogs need a 'job to do' in order to be fulfilled, happy companions. People create 'problem dogs' that fill shelters by asking them to fulfill human emotional needs! Many dogs are asked to be in alpha positions because humans do not understand the nature of the pack. A family is the 'pack' to the dog and the dog needs to understand their JOB in the pack. Truly, the only way dogs achieve the respect they deserve is when we allow them to be the creatures they were created to be.

Now I don't mean to put you off, but consider some factors please before you make this enormous decision. Just think of how awful it would be for a rescued Cavachon to be abandoned again because his owners could not cope! This **isn't a way of getting a cheap Cavachon** and going in with that mentality is so wrong. Even rescue centres may charge an admin fee but on top there are vaccinations, veterinary bills, worming, spaying or neutering to consider. Can you really afford these?

We asked **Linda & Steve Rogers of Timshell Farm**, are there things new owners do that perhaps frustrate you?

"It's rare, but if a family doesn't sign up for at least a few in-home training sessions, they always regret it! As you know, much easier to put a good habit in place than it is to correct a bad habit!"

Should You Get One or Two?

I believe that new owners should get ONE puppy at a time. The goal should be for the puppy to bond with his new owners - not each other. Admittedly, when you're sitting on the floor surrounded by frolicking Cavachon puppies, your heart may tell you to go ahead and get two. Listen to your head and not your heart!

Photo Credit: Kenneth Lang of Multiply Cavachons.

Owning one dog is a serious commitment of time and money, but with two dogs, everything doubles: food, housebreaking, training, vet bills, boarding fees, and time.

Pace yourself and start with one dog and put off buying a second for the future. Multiple Cavachon ownership is quite common, but especially if you are a first-time owner, you need to get accustomed to the Cavachon personality before taking on more than one.

Male or Female?

The only time gender is important is if you are intending to breed the dog. Otherwise, focus on the individual Cavachon's personality. In too many instances, people want female puppies because they assume they will be sweeter and gentler.

No valid basis exists for this assumption. Don't use such a **misconception** to reject a male dog. The real determining factor in any dog's long-term behavior is the quality of its training in relation to its place in the family. Consistency in addressing bad behaviors before they start is crucial.

Female dogs coddled as puppies display more negative behavior and greater territoriality than males. Consider this factor with a grown Cavachon, especially in a rescue situation.

A Cavachon's temperament needs to match the household to which it is going. So many owners want female puppies, but in many situations a neutered male is a much better fit.

When it comes to dogs like the Cavachon there are few physical distinctions between the sexes. The only difference you are likely to notice between a male and female Cavachon, in terms of physical characteristics, is that the female might be a little smaller than the male.

In terms of behavior, sometimes male Cavachons mature a little more slowly than females, so you might notice more puppy-like behavior from a male Cavachon puppy than a female once they reach 8 to 10 months of age. This might affect training – female Cavachons that develop faster than males become mature sooner and will likely respond to training better.

In general, you should spay or neuter your dog if you do not plan to breed it. Breeding your Cavachon is not a decision that you should make lightly and it is definitely not something you should do if your only reason is to make a profit.

Spaying female Cavachons before their first heat is believed to reduce the risk for ovarian cancer and other uterine diseases. Male Cavachons that are neutered tend to be less dominant than non-neutered male dogs – they may also be less likely to develop problem behaviors.

Melanie McCarthy of Cavachons From The Monarchy gives her opinion: "They are both equal in love, loyalty, training, friendliness, cheerfulness and most importantly, confidence.

"To find subtle differences between the genders, I look to 'pack behavior' in the wild. Females will focus on only one male in terms of breeding. Males will focus on all females available for breeding.

"What does this mean? It means that females can sometimes have a special fondness for one member of the family. Males do not.

"But this influence is so slight in a human family, one may not notice this, especially if all members of the family give the puppy lots of attention and interaction. I tell families that if they have a situation where one member of the family is gone all week, coming home on weekends only, they may want to consider a male who won't really 'notice' this absence during the week. I've only had this situation with a few families, where one spouse works out of town for the week and only comes home on the weekends. They chose a male for this reason."

Cost of Keeping a Cavachon

Being a pet owner is never cheap, especially if you stay up to date with vet appointments and feed your Cavachon a high-quality diet. Before you choose to buy or adopt a Cavachon you should make sure that you are able to comfortably cover all of the associated costs. When it comes to the cost of keeping a Cavachon you have to think about two different types of costs – upfront costs and ongoing costs.

Upfront costs are the costs you have to cover before you actually bring your Cavachon home. This includes things like your

Cavachon's crate, his food and water dishes, toys, grooming supplies, and the cost of the dog itself. Ongoing expenses include things like veterinary care, vaccinations, dog license, and food.

You will also need to pay for spay/neuter surgery, and microchipping is recommended. Spay/neuter surgery can be quite expensive if you go to a regular veterinary surgeon, but there are many low cost clinics that offer spay surgery for $100 to $200 and neuter surgery for as low as $50.

Photo Credit: Bailey from Jen Sweetman.

Having your Cavachon microchipped will cost you about $50, but it is well worth it. Each microchip has a unique number that is connected to a profile that includes your contact information. If your Cavachon gets lost, whoever finds him can take him to a shelter or vet to get the microchip scanned. Many animal shelters offer microchipping for as little as $15 or microchip them automatically before making them available for adoption.

In addition to the costs already mentioned, you will have to take your Cavachon in for regular visits to the vet. When he is a puppy you might have to go every few weeks for vaccinations, but after he turns 1 year old you'll only need to see the vet every 6 months.

Food is the other important recurring cost. Cavachons are small dogs so they do not eat a lot at one time. Bichon Frise dogs are particularly light eaters, so your Cavachon could be as well. While you might be able to find a month's supply of dog food for $15, you shouldn't skimp when it comes to your dog's diet. The quality of your Cavachon's diet will have a direct impact on his health and wellbeing, so you should choose a high-quality food, even if it costs a little bit more. Giving your dog a healthy diet will cut down on your veterinary costs in the long run because your dog will be healthier.

Chapter 4 – Buying a Cavachon

For many people who have never purchased a dog, the process can seem daunting and confusing. How do you select a breeder? How do you know if you're working with a good breeder? How do you pick a puppy? Are you paying a good price?

Photo Credit: Victoria Johnson of Cosmic Cavachons & Cavapoos.

How Much Do They Cost?

When it comes to buying a Cavachon you need to be very careful about the breeder you choose. Because hybrid dogs are so popular, inexperienced breeders may try to take advantage of unsuspecting pet parents – they might charge high prices for a 'designer dog' or bypass responsible breeding practices just to make a profit.

We have worked together with many of the top Cavachon breeders in producing this book. We asked them about their pricing and the consensus was that when looking at the price of a Cavachon, one must keep in mind all the costs incurred by a reputable breeder versus a puppy mill. No matter what the initial price, remember this is nothing compared to the long-term ongoing costs of dog ownership. Get a Cavachon who suffers health issues and that 'cheap' puppy is not so inexpensive after all.

A suspiciously low price means that Cavachon is most likely from a 'puppy mill' (think factory) where corners are cut, annual specialist exams do not happen, breeders continue to use parent dogs with genetic problems, and puppies are usually crated for the first 8 weeks and kept in isolation, meaning no socialisation, which could lead to behavioural problems that you get stuck with.

What is important is to ask the breeders about the **testing they do on the parent dogs,** and to ask what the guarantee is against health problems. Get this **in writing before you buy.** You need to base your decision on QUALITY and not price!

Before buying a Cavachon puppy you should look for several breeders and speak to them on the phone or in person, if possible. You should evaluate the breeder's knowledge not only of the breeding process but of the Cavachon breed specifically. When speaking to breeders you should avoid any that seem unwilling to answer your questions and those who do not seem to have the best interest of their puppies in mind. Never buy a Cavachon that is less than 8 weeks old or one that has not been fully weaned.

Most breeders do not list prices on their homepages, so you need to contact them directly. Good Cavachon breeders usually have a waiting list of prospective owners and **do not sell their dogs to anyone**. Of course it may be possible to browse the Internet or the local classified adverts and see lower prices, but **quality breeding comes at a cost** and if a Cavachon puppy is being sold for less, question why.

Sadly, unscrupulous breeders with almost no knowledge of the breed have sprung up, tempted by the prospect of making easy money. A healthy Cavachon will be an irreplaceable part of your family for the next decade or more. You shouldn't buy an unseen or imported puppy, or one from a pet shop or newspaper! You may end up saving a small amount in the short term only to find you have a puppy that has potential health issues which will cost you thousands more in the long run.

The Kennel Club has conducted research with shocking results. Too many people are still going to unscrupulous breeders, with:

• One third of people failing to see the puppy with its mother
• More than half not seeing the breeding environment
• 70% receive no contract of sale
• 82% not offered post-sales advice
• 69% not seeing any relevant health certificates for the puppy's parents, which indicate the likely health of the puppy

Obviously we have made clear that finding reputable breeders is your best way to find a puppy but these websites may also help:

American Kennel Club marketplace — http://marketplace.akc.org/
Adopt a Pet — http://www.adoptapet.com
Petango — http://www.petango.com
Puppy Find — http://www.puppyfind.com/
Oodle — http://dogs.oodle.com/

How to Choose a Breeder

Typically, the first step in finding a specific type of puppy is tracking down a breeder. Thankfully, this is hardly a problem with a breed as popular as the Cavachon. Visit breeder websites and speak over the phone to breeders in whose dogs you are interested. Ask them questions before you schedule a puppy visit. You want to be sure you are going to deal with a reputable breeder.

Some questions you should ask are:

1. Has the puppy been checked by a vet, and do they have a health certificate?
2. Has the puppy had shots and been wormed?
3. What health guarantee do you give with the puppy?

You want to arrive at a short list of potential breeders. Plan on visiting more than one before you make your decision. For now, know that your best option is to obtain a Cavachon from a breeder who is clearly serious about their breeding program and displays this fact with copious information about their dogs, including lots and lots of pictures.

Finding advertisements for Cavachons in local newspapers or similar publications is **dicey at best**. You may simply be dealing with a 'backyard breeder', a well-meaning person who has allowed the mating of two dogs of similar type. There is nothing inherently wrong with this situation, although I do strongly recommend that an independent veterinarian evaluates the puppy before purchase.

All too often, however, if you go through the classified ads you can stumble upon a puppy mill where dogs are being raised in deplorable conditions for profit only.

Never buy any dog unless you can meet the parents and siblings and see for yourself the surroundings in which the dog was born and is being raised. If you are faced with having to travel to pick up your dog, it's a huge advantage to see recorded video footage, or to do a live videoconference with the breeder and the puppies.

It is far, far preferable to work with a breeder from whom you can verify the health of the parents and discuss the potential for any congenital illnesses. Responsible breeders are more than willing to give you all this information and more, and are actively interested in making sure their dogs go to good homes. If you don't get this 'vibe' from someone seeking to sell you a dog, something is wrong.

I'm not a great fan of shipping live animals. If possible, try finding a local breeder, or one in reasonable traveling distance. Even if you find a Cavachon breeder online, visit the breeder at least once before you buy. Plan on picking your Cavachon up in person from the breeder.

Note that the Animal Care Welfare Act passed in November 2013 gives new laws/guidelines for breeders who ship. They now need to be **federally licensed** by the USDA.

Be suspicious of any breeder unwilling to allow such a visit or one who doesn't want to show you around their operation. You don't want to interact with just one puppy. You **should meet the parent(s) and the entire litter.**

It's important to get a sense of how the dogs live, and their level of care. When you talk to the breeder, information should flow in both directions. The breeder should discuss both the positives and negatives associated with the dogs.

Photo Credit: Jenna Lovatt of Pawfect Cavachons.

Nowadays many breeders are home-based and their dogs live in the house as pets. Puppies are typically raised in the breeder's home as well. It's very common for Cavachon breeders to use **guardian homes** for their breeding dogs. A guardian home is a permanent family for the dog. The breeder retains ownership of the dog during the years the dog is used for breeding, but the dog lives with the guardian family. This arrangement is great for the dog because once retired from breeding he/she is spayed/neutered and returned to its forever family. There is no need to re-home the dog after its breeding career has ended. There are still breeders who use kennels, but the number of home breeders is quite high and growing.

We asked **Linda Kaiser of Smooch My Pups** how she became a breeder: "I have been loving, raising, training animals most of my life. When I was a child I wanted to be a veterinarian. I have always been dedicated to be the best that I can be at anything I am passionate about. I was inspired to become serious about breeding when I acquired two champion Yorkshire Terriers about 15 years ago. Prior to that, I had raised and obedience trained Dobermans, but it wasn't something that I had planned to do forever. I didn't feel that way until I discovered the Cavachon hybrid. It has been pure love ever since, and I haven't looked back. This is a delightful, loving dog that loves everyone they meet."

What to Expect From a Good Breeder

Responsible breeders help you select a puppy. They place the long-term welfare of the dog front and center. The owner should show interest in your life and ask questions about your schedule, family, and other pets. This is not nosiness. It is an excellent sign that you are working with a professional with a genuine interest in placing their dogs appropriately. Owners who aren't interested in what kind of home the Cavachon will have are suspect.

When you go to look at puppies, take your lifestyle into consideration. Pick the puppy that will fit in your household. For example, if you have a quiet household and want a lap dog, or just want to take walks with the dog, pick the puppy with the laidback personality. They will be content to sit with you more. If you have active children and want a dog to play fetch with them, pick the busy puppy.

You want the breeder to be a resource for you in the future if you need help or guidance in living with your Cavachon. Be receptive to answering your breeder's queries and open to having an ongoing friendship.

It is quite common for breeders to call and check on how their dogs are doing and to make themselves available to answer questions.

I strongly recommend that you take your newly-purchased puppy to a vet to have a **thorough check-up within 48 hours**. If there are any issues with the health of the puppy, it will be difficult emotionally but worth it to return him to save you from a lifetime of pain as well as the financial costs in vet bills. Good breeders will have a guarantee for this eventuality in their contract.

Good Breeders Checklist

1. Check that the area where the puppies are kept is clean and that the puppies themselves look clean.

2. They don't breed multiple breeds: 2/3 maximum. Ideally they only breed and specialize in the Cavachon.

3. Their Cavachons are alert and appear happy and excited to meet you.

4. Puppies are not always available on tap but instead they have a waiting list of interested purchasers.

5. They don't over-breed, because this can be detrimental to the female's health.

6. They ask you lots of questions about you and your home.

7. They feed their Cavachons a high quality 'premium' dog food or possibly even a raw diet.

8. They freely offer great specific, detailed advice and indicate that they are on hand after the sale to help with any questions.

9. You get to meet the mother when you visit.

10. You are not rushed in and out, but get to spend time with the dogs and are able to revisit for a second time if necessary.

11. They provide a written contract and health guarantees.

12. They have health records for your puppy showing visits to the vet, vaccinations, worming, etc. and certificates to show

he is free from genetic defects.

13. They clearly explain what you need to do once you get your puppy home.

14. They agree to take the puppy back if necessary.

15. They are part of official organizations or have accreditations.

16. They have been breeding Cavachons for a number of years.

17. They allow you to speak to previous customers.

The Breeder Should Provide the Following

In the best cases, transactions with good breeders include the following components:

- The *contract of sale* details both parties' responsibilities. It also explains the transfer of paperwork and records.

- The *information packet* offers feeding, training, and exercise advice. It also recommends standard procedures like worming and vaccinations.

- The *description of ancestry* includes the names and types of Bichons and Cavalier King Charleses used in breeding.

- *Health records* detail medical procedures, include vaccination records, and disclose potential genetic issues.

- The breeder should *guarantee the puppy's health* at the time of pick up. You will be required to confirm this fact with a vet within a set period of time.

8 Warning Signs of a Potential Bad Breeder

Always be alert to key warning signs like:

1. Breeders who tell you it is not necessary for you to visit their facility in person.

2. Assertions that you can buy a puppy sight unseen with confidence.

3. Breeders who will allow you to come to their home or facility, but who will not show you where the dogs actually live.

4. Dogs kept in dirty, overcrowded conditions where the animals seem nervous and apprehensive.

5. Situations in which you are not allowed to meet at least one of the puppies' parents.

6. Sellers who can't produce health information or that say they will provide the records later.

7. No health guarantee and no discussion of what happens if the puppy does fall ill, including a potential refund.

8. Refusal to provide a signed bill of sale or vague promises to forward one later.

Avoiding Scams

No one wants to support a **puppy mill**. Such operations exist for profit only. They crank out the greatest number of litters possible with an eye toward nothing but the bottom line. The care the dogs receive ranges from deplorable to non-existent. Inbreeding is standard, leading to genetic abnormalities, wide-ranging health problems, and short lifespan. Puppy mills see Cavachons as profit, but give no thought to breeding integrity.

The Internet is, unfortunately, a ripe advertising ground for puppy mills, as are pet shops. If you can't afford to buy from a reputable breeder, consider a shelter or rescue dog: you are saving an animal in need.

Be **highly suspicious** of any breeder that assures you they have dogs available at all times. It is normal, and a sign that you are working with a reputable breeder, for your name to be placed on a waiting list. You may also be asked to place a small deposit to guarantee that you can buy a puppy from a coming litter. Should you choose not to take one of the dogs, this money is generally refunded, but find out the terms of such a transaction in advance.

Again, something is wrong if you can't:

- visit the facility where the puppies were born
- meet the parents
- inspect the facilities
- receive some genetic and health information

Identification Systems for Dogs

Your Cavachon may or may not have a means of permanent identification on their bodies when they are purchased. Governing organizations use differing systems. The American Kennel Club recommends permanent identification as a 'common sense' practice. The preferred options are tattoos or microchips.

Photo Credit: Nichola Lack of Cracking Cavachons.

Since 2016, microchipping is compulsory in the UK for all dogs. All puppies sold have to be microchipped by 8 weeks of age, i.e. prior to purchase by new owners.

Any dogs traveling to or returning to the UK from another country can do so under the Pet Passport system, for which microchipping is a requirement. For more information, see http://www.gov.uk/take-pet-abroad.

What is the Best Age to Purchase a Puppy?

Most Cavachon litters will have on average four or five puppies. Cavachon puppies are born with their eyes and ears closed. Newborn puppies have no teeth and very little fur, so they rely completely on their mother for warmth. Newborn pups weigh 6-8 oz on average.

A Cavachon puppy needs time to learn important life skills from the mother dog, including eating solid food and grooming themselves. For this reason, it is harmful to have puppies too early. These are the key puppy stages.

0-7 Weeks

Puppies typically open their eyes at 14 days and the ears will also open two weeks after birth. Puppies rely on their mothers not only for warmth during the first few weeks but also for food – they will spend about 90% of their day sleeping and 10% feeding.

Puppies live on a mother's milk-only diet for approximately the first 4 weeks. He learns discipline and manners from his mother, and littermates help with socialization and learning the social rules of the pack.

A mother will start to self-wean her pups when they are about four weeks old. You can tell when she is ready because she will not want to spend much time in the box with them. As the puppies' teeth emerge, the dam will be more reluctant to nurse. This is normal and helps her milk production start to slow down. At this point it is important for the breeder to start supplementing the puppies with a good quality puppy food mixture four times per day. Usually by seven or eight weeks the puppies are fully weaned from the mother's milk.

Puppies are not able to control their bowels when they are first born so the mother will lick them to help stimulate urination and defecation.

8-12 Weeks

At about eight weeks the puppies will receive their first vaccine. Because it is not known exactly when the maternal antibodies from the mother's milk will wear off, a series of vaccines is required. Your veterinarian will give you the best recommendations.

The fact is that most puppies go home at eight weeks, but none

should ever go sooner than this as this could result in negative issues such as shyness. A 'breeder' doing this may simply want to cash in and turn over lots of puppies too quickly.

Photo Credit: Jenna Lovatt of Pawfect Cavachons.

From the time the puppies are weaned at about eight weeks, until they are ready for their new homes, their mother and siblings continue to teach them 'dog manners'. A good breeder will also start basic leash and crate training during the first 8-12 week. This helps the puppy adjust to its new home much easier!

Now that the brain is developed, he needs socializing with the outside world, otherwise he can become fearful.

12 Weeks Onwards

Some breeders will insist on keeping the puppies longer (10-12 weeks) to allow the puppy's immune system to become stronger.

During your puppy's change to adolescence, continue exposure to as many different sounds, smells, and people as possible. Begin formal training and obedience, and always praise his good behavior without being too strict or too soft with him.

How to Choose a Puppy?

My best advice is to go with the puppy that is drawn to you. My standard strategy in selecting a pup has always been to sit a little apart from a litter and let one of the dogs come to me. My late father was, in his own way, a 'dog whisperer'. He taught me this trick for picking puppies, and it's never let me down.

I've had dogs in my life since childhood and enjoyed a special connection with them all. I will say that often the dog that comes to me isn't the one I might have chosen — but I still consistently rely on this method.

You will want to choose a puppy with a friendly, easy-going temperament, and your breeder should be able to help you with

your selection. Also ask the breeder about the temperament and personalities of the puppy's parents and if they have socialized the puppies.

Photo Credit: Fifi from Pat Kelleher.

Always be certain to ask if a Cavachon puppy you are interested in has displayed any signs of aggression or fear, because if this is happening at such an early age, you may experience behavioral troubles as the puppy becomes older.

Beyond this, I suggest that you interact with your dog with a clear understanding that **each one is an individual** with unique traits. It is not so much a matter of learning about all Cavachons, but rather of learning about YOUR Cavachon dog.

9 Essential Health Tests You Can Use

Before the 'Aw Factor' kicks in and you are completely swept away by the cuteness of a Cavachon puppy, familiarize yourself with some basic quick health checks.

1. Although a puppy may be sleepy at first, the dog should wake up quickly and be both alert and energetic.

2. The little dog should feel well fed in your hands, with some fat over the rib area.

3. The coat should be shiny and healthy with no dandruff, bald patches, or greasiness.

4. The puppy should walk and run easily and energetically with no physical difficulty or impairment.

5. The eyes should be bright and clear with no sign of discharge or crustiness.

6. Breathing should be quiet, with no sneezing or coughing and no discharge or crust on the nostrils.

7. Examine the area around the genitals to ensure there is no visible fecal collection or accumulation of pus. If a puppy is dirty from pee or fecal matter then that, for me, is reason to leave quickly without wasting any more of your time, as it indicates poor standards.

8. Test the dog's hearing by clapping your hands when the puppy is looking away from you and judge the puppy's reaction.

9. Test the vision by rolling a ball toward the dog, making sure the puppy appropriately notices and interacts with the object.

6 Great Checks for Puppy Social Skills

When choosing a puppy out of a litter, look for one that is friendly and outgoing, rather than one who is overly aggressive or fearful. Puppies who demonstrate good social skills with their littermates are much more likely to develop into easy-going, happy adult dogs that play well with others.

Observe all the puppies together and take notice:

1. Which puppies are comfortable both on top and on the bottom when play fighting and wrestling with their littermates? Which puppies seem to only like being on top?

2. Which puppies try to keep the toys away from the other puppies, and which puppies share?

3. Which puppies seem to like the company of their littermates, and which ones seem to be loners?

4. Puppies that ease up or stop rough play when another puppy yelps or cries are more likely to respond appropriately when they play too roughly as adults.

5. Is the puppy sociable with humans? If they will not come to you, or display fear toward strangers, this could develop into a problem later in their life.

6. Is the puppy relaxed about being handled? If not, they may become difficult with adults and children during daily interactions, grooming, or visits to the veterinarian's office.

Submissive or Dominant?

It is something of a myth that dogs are either submissive or dominant. In reality, they are likely to be somewhere in between the two, but it is helpful to understand where they fit in so you know how to deal with them. Watching how they act around their littermates can give you clues.

Submissive dogs:

- Turn away when other dogs stare
- Are happy to play with their littermates
- Do not try to dominate other dogs
- May show submissive urination when greeting other dogs
- Allow other dogs to win at tug-of-war
- Provide attention and affection to other dogs
- Back off when other dogs want to take food or toys
- Roll on their backs to display their belly

If a Cavachon shows definite submissive or dominant tendencies, which should you pick? There is no one right answer. You need to choose a puppy that best suits your family's lifestyle.

A submissive Cavachon will naturally be more passive, less manic, and possibly easier to train. A dominant Cavachon will usually be more energetic and lively. They could be more stubborn and difficult to train or socialize, but this needn't be a negative and can be overcome with a little persistence.

Dogs are pack animals, and they are happiest when they have structure and they can follow their nature. Followers want to be told what to do and know what the leaders expect of them. Know that you must be the pack leader to your Cavachon. He should be submissive even to younger children, so aggression and other problem behaviors don't arise.

Photo: Melanie McCarthy of Cavachons From The Monarchy.

Linda & Steve Rogers of Timshell Farm want to help you make the right choice:

"It's so easy to get emotionally charged up about getting a beautiful puppy, and getting really hooked by photos on a website. But, sadly, we get many calls from people that have done just that, and (have) ended up with a puppy that had to be put down because of a serious heart defect, or have extremely expensive surgery to correct patellar luxation, and the breeders offered no refund, full or partial. You can breed for puppies with sound health using parent dogs that have been screened for genetic faults prior to being bred, or not.

"We get calls from people that paid a lot for a puppy only to discover it has temperament disorders that cannot be corrected, after spending many thousands of dollars with professional trainers. This is all so avoidable.

"People need to know about the health guarantee the breeder offers. What does it cover? All genetic faults? Do you have to return the puppy to the breeder as part of the health guarantee? This is how many breeders get out of honoring their guarantee. They know the buyer will be way too attached to the puppy to return it, in order to get the refund. The refund should go towards the cost of surgery to repair the patella, etc. or whatever health fault needs medical attention. So, you shouldn't have to return your puppy as part of the guarantee.

"Always buy from a breeder that has verifiable references from professional trainers, previous adoptive families, or vets. Do a search on the Better Business Bureau website to confirm that the business has no complaints or has settled all complaints.

"Verify the breeder's reputation by speaking with other families that have adopted puppies from them to make sure the puppies come from quality adult breeding dogs and that the breeder is honest and ethical. Ask to see the buyer's contract and health warranty documents BEFORE you buy. Go by contract and not just conversation.

"Deal directly with your breeder and avoid any middlemen. When considering any business, BE SURE to do a Google search for the business or the website name followed by the words 'complaints' or 'reviews'. If there have been problems, various websites for rip-off reporting and consumer complaints will come up."

Chapter 5 – Caring for Your New Puppy

All puppies are forces of nature. That's especially true for an exuberant, sweet, curious, happy, hyperactive, chewing, barking Cavachon! They are little dogs that can get in big trouble before you even know what's happened. The first job ahead of you – and I do mean *before* you bring your new pet home – is to puppy proof the house!

Litter of Ruby Cavachons from Melanie McCarthy of Cavachons From The Monarchy.

Identify the Dangers

Think of a puppy as a bright toddler with four legs. Get yourself in the mindset that you're bringing a baby genius home, and try to think like a puppy. Every nook and cranny invites exploration. A puppy's inquisitive nose goes into every crevice. Every discovery is then chewed, swallowed – or both!

A Cavachon, especially a young one, will eat pretty much anything, often gulping something down with no forethought.

Take a complete inventory of the areas to which the dog will have access. Remove all lurking poisonous dangers from cabinets and shelves. Get everything up and out of the dog's reach.

If you are not sure about any item, it is best to assume it's poisonous and remove it. Pay special attention to:

- cleaning products
- insecticides
- mothballs
- fertilizers
- antifreeze

Get down on the floor and have a look around from puppy level. Your new furry Einstein will spot anything that catches your attention and many things that don't!

Do not leave any dangling electrical cords, drapery pulls, or even loose scraps of wallpaper. Look for forgotten items that have gotten wedged behind cushions or kicked under the furniture. Don't let anything stay out that is a **potential choking hazard**.

Tie up anything that could be a 'topple' danger. A coaxial cable may look boring to you, but in the mouth of a determined little dog, it could bring a heavy television set crashing down. Cord minders and electrical ties are your friends!

Remove stuffed items and pillows, and cover the legs of prized pieces of furniture against chewing. Take anything out of the room that even looks like it *might* be a toy. Think I'm kidding? Go online and do a Google image search for 'dog chewed cell phone' and shudder at what you will see.

Bowel blockages can occur from a Cavachon eating foreign objects they cannot pass. Some Cavachons are chewers. You must be careful about leaving things on the floor or within reach of them. Rope toys, some hard plastic or rubber bones, towels, or any material with string can be deadly to a dog. I stopped using towels as bedding many years ago as one dog ate part of a towel and could not pass it. The string acts like a saw in the intestines. This can be deadly.

If you suspect your pup or dog has eaten something, call your vet immediately as this could require surgery. Your vet may instruct you to induce vomiting to get it up first. If you see that your dog has no interest in eating, or eats and vomits, it could have a blockage. They may be lethargic. They may also have a tender belly if you rub it. All these are reason for concern. I recommend replacing bedding with fleece blankets. They have no string and if a dog chews it up it will pass the material.

Plants Can Be Lethal

The list of indoor and outdoor plants that are a toxic risk to dogs is long (over 700!) and includes many surprises. You may know that apricot and peach pits are poisonous to canines, but what about spinach and tomato vines?

The American Society for the Prevention of Cruelty to Animals has created a large reference list of plants for dog owners, available at: https://www.aspca.org/pet-care/animal-poison-control/toxic-and-non-toxic-plants

Go through the list and remove any plants from your home that might make your puppy sick. Don't think for a minute that your Cavachon will leave such items alone. He won't!

What to Call Your Cavachon?

Have you thought of a name yet? Here are our best breeder tips:

1. Choose something you're not embarrassed to shout out loud in public.
2. The shorter the better. Dogs find names with 1 or 2 syllables easiest to recognize, e.g. Lucky.
3. Long names inevitably end up being shortened so think what they could be now — do you like them?
4. Names starting with s, sh, ch, k, etc. are good because dogs hear high frequency sounds best.
5. Ending with a vowel works well, particularly a short 'a' or a long 'e' sound.

6. Avoid popular and cliché names.
7. Don't go for a name that sounds similar to a command.
8. If you take ownership of a Cavachon that already has a name, keep the new one similar sounding for his sake.

Bringing Your "Baby" Home

Before you bring your new puppy home, buy an appropriate travel crate and a wire crate for home use. Since the home crate will also be an important tool in housebreaking, the size of the unit is important.

Many pet owners want to get a crate large enough for the puppy to 'grow into' in the interest of saving money. When you are housebreaking a dog, you are working with the principle that the animal will not soil its own 'den'. If you buy a huge crate for a small dog, the puppy is likely to pick a corner as the 'bathroom', thus setting back his training.

For Cavachons, a good **travel crate size** is the 200 series crate, which measures 28" x 20.5" x 21.5".

For the **wire-crate for home use** we recommend the Midwest Two-door Crate Model 15244 DD 24" x 18" x 19" (or similar size from another manufacturer).

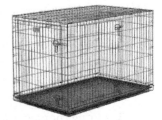

Put one or two puppy-safe chew toys in the crate for the ride home, along with a recently worn article of clothing. You want the dog to learn your scent. Be sure to fasten the seat belt over the crate.

Talk to the breeder to ensure your Cavachon doesn't eat too close to the journey so there is less chance of car sickness, and when he arrives at your home he will be hungry — always a good start!

It is also a nice touch to get an **old rag or towel** from your breeder that has been with the dam. Leave this with your puppy for the first few days, as her scent will help him to settle in more easily.

Take your puppy out to do its business before putting it in the crate. Expect whining and crying. **Don't give in!** Leave them in the crate! It's far safer for the puppy to ride there than to be on someone's lap. Try if possible to take someone with you to sit next to the crate and comfort the puppy while you drive.

Don't overload the dog's senses with too many people. No matter how excited the kids may be at the prospect of a new puppy, leave the children back at the house. The trip home needs to be calm and quiet.

You may need to make a stop, depending on the length of journey. He will likely be nervous, so cover the bottom of the crate with newspapers or a towel just in case. **Have water** and give him a drink en route.

As soon as you arrive home, take your Cavachon puppy to a patch of grass outside so he can relieve himself. Immediately **begin encouraging** him for doing so. Dogs are pack animals with an innate desire to please their 'leader'. Positive and consistent praise is an important part of housebreaking.

Although a gregarious breed, Cavachons can easily be overwhelmed and nervous in new surroundings. This is especially true of a puppy away from its mother and littermates for the first time. Stick with the usual feeding schedule, and use the same kind of food the dog has been receiving at the breeder's, because their digestive systems cannot cope with a sudden change.

Create a designated 'puppy safe' area in the house and let the puppy explore on its own. Don't isolate the little dog, but don't overwhelm it either. Resist the urge to pick up the puppy every time it cries.

Give the dog soft pieces of worn clothing to further familiarize him with your scent. Leave a radio playing at a low volume for 'company'. At night you may opt to give the baby a well-wrapped warm water bottle, but put the dog in its crate and do not bring it to bed with you.

I realize that last bit may sound all but impossible, but if you want a crate-trained dog, you have to **start from day one**. It's much, much harder to get a dog used to sleeping overnight in his crate after any time in the bed with you.

I also suggest you **take some time off work**. For about two weeks this will be your full-time job! Constant supervision is essential to housetrain your puppy quickly and to give him company while he gets accustomed to his new home, which can be overwhelming to begin with.

Photo Credit: Linda Kaiser of Smooch My Pups.

Remember that your new puppy is essentially a newborn baby — they need a lot of sleep! Puppies need their nap time, especially after playing. Also, in the evening keep them up with you so when you are ready to go to bed the pup is as well.

It is also likely for them to whine for the first few days as they adapt to their new surroundings, and they may well follow you around the house constantly. Just handle them gently, make them comfortable and give them peace and quiet and allow them to sleep as much as they need.

They may also shiver and not eat. Of course, this is all very stressful for you, but don't panic. Obviously ensure they are not in a cold place, and put warm blankets in their crate or bed. Your Cavachon will eat eventually. Try taking the food away if they are not ready to eat, then the next time you put something down for him, he is more likely to be hungry.

The Importance of the Crate

The crate plays an important role in your dog's life. Historically crates have been more popular in America than in Europe, however, this attitude is slowly changing. Don't think of its use as 'imprisoning' your Cavachon. The dog sees the crate as a den and will retreat to it for safety and security. Cavachons often go to their crates just to enjoy quiet time like we humans do from time to time!

When you accustom your dog to a crate as a puppy, you **get ahead** of issues of separation anxiety and prepare your pet to do well with travel. The crate also plays an important role in housebreaking, a topic we will discuss shortly.

Never rush crate training. Don't lose your temper or show frustration. The Cavachon must go into the crate on its own. Begin by leaving the door open. Tie it in place so it does not slam shut by accident. Give your puppy a treat each time he goes inside. Reinforce his good behavior with verbal praise.

Never use the crate as punishment. Proper use of the crate gives both you and your Cavachon peace of mind. In time with some patience and training, he will regard the crate **as his special place** in the house.

Melanie McCarthy of Cavachons From The Monarchy: "We recommend two crates, one within earshot of inside the bedroom of a family member and then the other crate in a medium traffic area on the main floor. We use specific crates because you want one that comes with a divider; we block off 2/3 of the crate and only use 1/3. If you don't do this, the puppy goes to the corner and pees and poops there, totally stopping progress for potty training."

Linda & Steve Rogers of Timshell Farm recommend a product called Snuggle Puppy: "They are great for calming the puppy in the crate – couple that with a covered crate and the puppy goes right to sleep. Exercise, covered crate and Snuggle Puppy = sound asleep puppy in under two minutes!"

From SmartPetLove.com: "Our products incorporate the real-feel pulsing heartbeat technology and warmth to help soothe your pet."

Keely Wilkins of Ballyhara: "Crate training is an absolute must for all puppies; in my opinion it makes better adjusted and well-rounded puppies. I find that house training and the time it takes to complete house training greatly depends on the owner and how consistent they are with their training. If they're greatly inconsistent they will find it much more difficult to house train their puppy."

Here are our top 10 crate training tips:

1. Cavachons like to be near their family, so initially he will whine and cry simply because he is separated from you and not because he is in 'a cage'. Remember that any sort of interaction, positive or negative, will be a 'reward' to him, so ignore the whining.

2. Give your Cavachon enough room to turn around in. They appreciate space.

3. Always ensure there is access to fresh water inside the crate.

4. Don't keep them locked up in their crate all day just because you have to go to work — this is unfair.

5. Young puppies shouldn't spend more than 2-3 hours in the crate without a toilet break as they cannot last that long without relieving themselves. This means you should take them out for toilet breaks during the night.

6. Don't place the crate in a draughty place or in direct sunlight where he could overheat. A constant temperature is best. A metal wire crate (compared to plastic) is best so air flows through the gaps.

7. Making the crate his bed from day one is best. Put in some bedding so he feels comfortable and warm at night.

8. Initially to crate train him, put some tasty treats in the crate and leave the door open when he dashes in excitedly! Also be sure to feed him his meals in the crate so he associates it with positive emotions. Don't shut the door yet as that will introduce a negative aspect. Let him roam in and out, being rewarded with treats when he goes into the crate.

9. After a few days, you can begin closing the door for short periods while he is eating. Get ready for some possible whining but remember to stay strong! Some treats pushed through the wire as a reward works well.

10. To begin with, just close the door for a minute, no more. In a few days, increase the time gradually so he slowly gets accustomed to the door being closed.

Jen Sweetman, owner of Bailey says: "Personally, I recommend crate training, especially when children are living in the same house as it can, at times, be very noisy. Bailey's crate is always open and he knows that if he wants a bit of peace or quiet time, he can go in there, be left alone and come out when he's ready."

Where Should They Sleep?

I have established that I am firmly behind the use of a crate, but you can also have a bed if you prefer, but most importantly — where will they sleep?

I know some new Cavachon owners can't resist having them in their beds, but I strongly suggest not giving into this! Yes, they will whine and cry for the first couple of nights but **this will stop!** Sleeping in your bed could be dangerous: they might wet the bed, and with their relatively short legs **it is potentially dangerous** for them to jump on and off the bed.

I don't recommend it but yes, you could have the crate in the bedroom initially, but why not just start as you mean to go on from day one? Place the crate downstairs I say, and your life will be so much easier once they settle in after a few days.

Photo Credit: Bailey from Jen Sweetman.

Go Slow With the Children and Pets

If you have children, talk to them before the puppy arrives. Explain that the little dog will be nervous and scared being away from its mother and old home. The initial transition is important. Supervise all interactions for everyone's safety and comfort.

Help children understand how to handle the puppy and to carry it safely. **Limit playtime** until everyone gets to know each other. In just a matter of days, your Cavachon puppy will be romping with your kids.

Introductions with other pets, especially with cats, often boil down to matters of territoriality. All dogs, by nature, defend their territory against intruders. This instinct is strong in Cavachons.

Don't let a Cavachon puppy and a cat meet face-to-face without some preparation. Create a neutral and controlled interaction under a closed bathroom door first. Since cats are 'weaponized' with an array of razor sharp claws, Fluffy can quickly put a puppy in his place. Of course, you want to oversee the first 'in-person' meeting, but don't overreact. Let the animals sort it out.

With other dogs in the house, you may want a more hands-on approach to the first 'meet and greet'. Always have two people present to control each dog. Make the introduction in a place that the older dog does not regard as 'his'. Even if the two dogs are going to be living in the same house, let them meet in neutral territory.

Keep your tone and demeanor calm, friendly, and happy. Let the dogs conduct the usual 'sniff test', but don't let it go on for too long. Either dog may consider lengthy sniffing to be aggression. Puppies may not yet understand the behavior of an adult dog and can be absolute little pests.

If this is what is going on, do not scold the older dog for issuing a warning snarl or growl. A well-socialized older dog won't be displaying aggression under such circumstances. He's just putting junior in his place and establishing the hierarchy of the pack.

Be careful when you bring a new dog into the house **not to neglect the older dog**. Also be sure to spend time with him away from the puppy to assure your existing pet that your bond with him is strong and intact.

Exercise caution at mealtimes. Feed your pets in separate bowls so there is no perceived competition for food. (This is also a good policy to follow when introducing your puppy to the family cat.)

What Can I Do to Make My Cavachon Love Me?

From the moment you bring your Cavachon dog home, every minute you spend with him is an opportunity to bond.

Have in mind that your Cavachon has left the warmth and security of his mother and littermates, so initially for a few days he will be confused and even sad. It is important to make the transition from the birth home to your home as easy as possible.

The earlier you start working with your dog, the more quickly that bond will grow and the closer you and your Cavachon will become.

While simply spending time with your Cavachon will encourage the growth of that bond, there are a few things you can do to purposefully build your bond with your dog. Some of these things include:

- **Engaging** your Cavachon in games like fetch and hide-and-seek to encourage interaction.

- Taking your Cavachon for **daily walks**, during which you frequently stop to pet and talk to your dog. Allow your puppy time to sniff and smell on their walks. He is a hound and loves to explore new scents.

- Interacting with your dog through **daily training sessions** – teach your dog to pay attention when you say his name.

- Being calm and consistent when training your dog – always use **positive reinforcement** rather than punishment.

- Spending **as much time** with your Cavachon as possible, even if it means simply keeping the dog in the room with you while you cook dinner or pay bills.

Common Mistakes to Avoid

Never pick your Cavachon puppy up if they are showing fear or aggression toward an object, another dog, or person, because this will be rewarding them for unbalanced behavior.

If they are doing something you do not want them to continue, your puppy needs to be gently corrected by you with firm and calm energy, so that they learn not to react with fear or aggression. When the mum of the litter tells her puppies off, she will use a deep noise with strong eye contact, until the puppy quickly realizes it's doing something naughty.

Don't play the 'hand' game, where you slide the puppy across the floor with your hands, because it's amusing for humans to see a little ball of fur scrambling to collect themselves and run back across the floor for another go.

This sort of 'game' will teach your puppy to disrespect you as their leader in two different ways — first, because this 'game' teaches them that humans are their play toys, and secondly, this type of 'game' teaches them that humans are a source of excitement. A Cavachon is NOT a toy!

When your Cavachon puppy is teething, they will naturally want to chew on everything within reach, and this will include you. As cute as you might think it is when they are young puppies, this is not an acceptable behavior, and you need to gently, but firmly, discourage the habit, just like a mother dog does to her puppies when they need to be weaned.

Always **praise your puppy** when they stop inappropriate behavior, as this is the beginning of teaching them to understand rules and boundaries. Often we humans are quick to discipline a puppy or dog for inappropriate behavior, but we forget to praise them for their good behavior.

Don't treat your Cavachon like a small, furry human. When people **try to turn dogs into people**, this can cause them much stress and confusion that could lead to behavioral problems.

A well-behaved Cavachon **thrives on rules and boundaries**, and when they understand that there is no question you are their leader and they are your follower, they will live a contented, happy and stress-free life.

Dogs are a different species with different rules; for example, they do not naturally cuddle, and they need to learn to be stroked and cuddled by humans. Therefore, be careful when approaching a dog for the first time and being overly expressive with your hands. The safest areas to touch are the back and chest — avoid patting on the head and touching the ears.

Many people will assume that a dog that is yawning is tired — this is often a misinterpretation, and instead the dog is signaling that he is uncomfortable and nervous about a situation.

Be careful when **staring at dogs** because this is one of the ways in which they threaten each other. This body language can make them feel distinctly uneasy.

Habituation and Socialization

Habituation is when you continuously provide exposure to the same stimuli over a period of time. This will help your Cavachon to relax in his environment and will teach him how to behave around unfamiliar people, noises, other pets, and different surroundings. Expose your Cavachon puppy continuously to new sounds and new environments.

When you allow for your Cavachon to face life's positive experiences through socialization and habituation, you're helping your Cavachon to build a library of valuable information that he can use when he's faced with a difficult situation. If he's had plenty of wonderful and positive early experiences, the more likely he'll be able to bounce back from any surprising or scary experiences.

When your Cavachon puppy arrives at his new home for the first time, he'll start bonding with his human family immediately. This will be his **primary** bond. His **secondary** bond will be with everyone outside your home. A dog should never be secluded inside his home. Be sure to find the right balance, where you're not exposing your Cavachon puppy to too much external stimuli.

If he starts becoming fearful, speak to your veterinarian. The puppyhood journey can be tiresome yet very rewarding. Primary socialization starts between three and five weeks of age, when a

pup's experiences take place within his litter. This will have a huge impact on all his future emotional behavior.

Photo Credit: Bob from Natalie Mayatt.

Socialization from six to twelve weeks allows for puppies to bond with other species outside of their littermates and parents. It's at this particular stage that most pet parents will bring home a puppy and where he'll soon become comfortable with humans, other pets, and children.

By the time a puppy is around twelve to fourteen weeks, he becomes more difficult to introduce to new environments and new people and starts showing suspicion and distress.

Nonetheless, if you've recently bought a Cavachon puppy or are bringing one home and he's beyond this ideal age, don't neglect to continue the socialization process. Puppies need to be exposed to as many new situations, environments, people, and other animals as possible, and **it is never too late to start.**

During puppyhood, you can easily teach your puppy to politely greet a new person, yet by the time a puppy has reached social maturity, the same puppy, if not properly socialized, may start lunging forward and acting aggressively, with the final outcome of lunging and nipping.

Never accidentally reward your Cavachon puppy for displaying fear or growling at another dog or animal by picking them up. Picking up a Cavachon puppy or dog at this time, when they are displaying unbalanced energy, actually turns out **to be a reward for them**, and you will be teaching them to continue with this type of behavior. As well, picking up a puppy literally places them in a 'top dog' position where they are higher and more dominant than the dog or animal they just growled at.

The correct action to take in such a situation is to gently correct your puppy with a firm yet calm energy by distracting them with a 'No', so that they learn to let you deal with the situation on their behalf.

If you allow a fearful or nervous puppy to deal with situations that unnerve them all by themselves, they may learn to react with fear or aggression, and you will have created a problem that could escalate into something quite serious as they grow older.

The same is true of situations where a young puppy may feel the need to protect themselves from a bigger or older dog that may come charging in for a sniff. It is the guardian's responsibility to protect the puppy so that they do not think they must react with fear or aggression in order to protect themselves.

Once your Cavachon puppy has received all their vaccinations, you can take them out to public dog parks and various locations where many dogs are found.

Before allowing them to interact with other dogs or puppies, take them for a disciplined walk on leash so that they will be a little tired and less likely to immediately engage with all other dogs.

Keep your puppy on leash and close beside you, because most puppies are usually a bundle of out-of-control energy, and **you need to protect them** while teaching them how far they can go before getting themselves into trouble with adult dogs who may not appreciate excited puppy playfulness.

If your puppy shows any signs of aggression or domination toward another dog, you must **immediately step in** and calmly discipline them.

Take your puppy everywhere with you and introduce them to many different people of all ages, sizes, and ethnicities. Most people will come to you and want to interact with your puppy. If they ask if they can hold your puppy, let them, because so long as they are gentle and don't drop the puppy, this is a good way to socialize your Cavachon and show them that humans are friendly.

As important as socialization is, it is also important that your Cavachon be left alone for short periods when young so that they can cope with some periods of isolation. If an owner goes out and they have never experienced this, they can destroy things or make a mess because of panic. They are thinking they are vulnerable and can be attacked by something or someone coming into the house.

Safety First

Never think for a minute that your Cavachon would not bolt and run away. Even well-adjusted, happy puppies and adult dogs can run away, usually in extreme conditions such as during fireworks, thunder, or when scared.

If he gets lost, it is important he can be identified:

1. Get him a collar with an ID tag because some people may presume that dogs without collars have been abandoned. Note that hanging tags can get caught on things.

2. Put your phone number but not his name on the tag in case he is stolen. A thief will then not be able to use his name. Consider saying, 'for reward, call...'.

3. Inserting a microchip below the skin via injection is

recommended as this cannot be removed easily by a thief.

4. Recent photos of your Cavachon with the latest clip need to be placed in your wallet or purse.

Train your Cavachon – foster and work with a professional, positive trainer to ensure that your dog does not run out the front door or out the backyard gate. Teach your Cavachon basic, simple commands such as 'come' and 'stay'.

Create a special, fun digging area just for him, hide his bones and toys, and let your Cavachon know that it's okay to dig in that area. After all, dogs need to play!

Introduce your new, furry companion to all your neighbors so everyone will know that he belongs to you.

Know that your Cavachon will not instinctively be fearful of cars so be very careful around roads.

Your Puppy's First Lessons

Don't give a young Cavachon full run of the house before it is housetrained. Keep your new pet confined to a designated area behind a baby gate. This protects your home and possessions and keeps the dog safe from hazards like staircases. Depending on the size and configuration, baby gates retail from $25-$100 / £15-£60.

Melanie McCarthy of Cavachons From The Monarchy: "Personally we don't recommend baby gates because puppies will still chew the bottom of cabinets and chew and destroy electrical cords, rugs on a floor, bottom of chairs. Far better is an exercise pen – Midwest makes great ones that fold up easily or fold into any shape you want and you can attach the wire crates to them."

Chapter 6 - Housetraining

This section covers the all-important training of your Cavachon to go relieve themselves outside. This is referred to as housebreaking or housetraining and in America it is often referred to as **potty training**.

If you are fortunate and the breeder has done their job, the puppy should already have a basic understanding of what is expected with potty training. A puppy that has been allowed to soil his sleeping area or go wherever they are will be far more difficult to house train than one who has been taken out routinely and encouraged to potty outside.

New owners always ask me how long it will take - there is no timetable for a dog being totally house trained. Yes, it can be as quick as two weeks but each pup is an individual and some pick up

faster than others. Patience, being consistent in taking them out, and praise when they go are the keys to success. Also, take note on the times the pup needs to go out. This is helpful with taking them out on their schedule.

Photo Credit: Linda & Steve Rogers of Timshell Farm.

Jen Sweetman, owner of Bailey, had this experience: "Toilet training with Bailey did take some time; he was about 7 months old when fully toilet trained. I am aware of many more that have been trained much earlier though. I bought some training bells eventually, following recommendations on a Facebook group, which he got the hang of very quickly and still uses them now."

Barby Wolfish of Pet Pointe: "I had heard that Cavachons can be difficult to house train but we did not find that to be the case. As with any training, consistency seems to be the key when training these dogs."

When the Cavachon is born, they relieve themselves inside their den, with the mother cleaning them up so there is never a scent of urine or feces where the puppies eat, sleep, and live. As they get older, they follow their mother's lead in learning to go outside, so housetraining may already be established when you take your puppy home. If not, they are probably well on the way already. They just need some extra guidance from you.

We have already stressed the importance of being at home for the first two weeks at least when you bring your pup back from the breeder. If he is left on his own, expect him to eliminate inside the house because at this stage he doesn't realize that the whole house is in effect his den and not the place to eliminate.

Crate training and housebreaking go hand in hand. Cavachons, like all dogs, come to **see their crate as their den**. They will hold their need to urinate or defecate while they are inside.

Establishing and maintaining a daily routine also helps your dog in this respect. Feed your Cavachon at the same time each day, taking him out afterwards. The feeding schedule dictates the frequency of 'relief' breaks. Trips 'out' will also decrease as the dog ages.

Don't be rigid in holding your puppy to this standard. Puppies have less control over their bladder and bowel movements than adult Cavachons. They need to go out more often, especially after they've been active or have become excited.

On average, adult dogs go **out 3-4 times a day**: when they wake up, within an hour of eating, and right before bedtime. With puppies, don't wait more than 15 minutes after a meal.

If you are keeping your Cavachon puppy in a crate overnight, he will need to be let out once or twice a night, as he will not be able to hold it in the whole night until he is aged about four or five months old.

Getting your Cavachon puppy to go outside from day one is best. Your Cavachon will want to keep eliminating in the same spot because the scent acts as **a signal 'to go'** in their mind. In time this spot becomes safe and familiar to them. Don't allow them to go on your lawn; being soft, they like this because it feels good under their paws. A discreet corner furthest away from your back door is best, perhaps an area of gravel or, if you live in an apartment, you can use a dog litter tray.

Praise your Cavachon with the same phrases to encourage and reinforce good elimination habits. NEVER punish him for having an accident. There is no association in his mind with the punishment and the incident. He'll have an uncomfortable awareness that he's done *something* to make you unhappy, but **he won't know what.**

Getting upset or scolding a puppy for having an accident inside the home is the wrong approach, because this will result in teaching your puppy to be afraid of you and to only relieve themselves in secret places or when you're not watching.

If you catch your Cavachon puppy making a mistake, all that is necessary is for you to calmly say 'no', and take them outside or to their indoor bathroom area. Resist the temptation to scoop him up because he needs to learn to walk to the door himself when he needs to go outside.

Clean up the accident using an enzymatic cleaner to eradicate the odor and return to the dog's normal routine.

Nature's Miracle Stain and Odor Removal is an excellent product and affordable at $5 / £2.97 per 32 ounce / 0.9 liter bottle.

I'm not a big fan of puppy pads because I find puppies like the softness of the pads, which can encourage them to eliminate on other soft areas — such as your carpets!

The following are methods that you may or may not have

considered, all of which have their own merits, including:

• Bell training
• Exercise pen training
• Kennel training

All of these are effective methods, so long as you add in the one critical and often missing 'wild card' ingredient, which is 'human training'.

When you bring home your new Cavachon puppy, they will be relying upon your guidance to teach them what they need to learn, and when it comes to housetraining, the first thing the human guardian needs to learn is that the puppy is not being bad when they pee or poop inside.

They are just responding to the call of Mother Nature, and you need to pay close attention right from the very beginning. If your puppy is making bathroom 'mistakes', blame yourself, not your puppy.

Check in with yourself and make sure your energy remains consistently calm and patient, and that you exercise plenty of compassion and understanding while you help your new puppy learn the bathroom rules. Don't clean up after your puppy with them watching, as this makes the puppy believe you are there to clean up after them, making you lower in the dog pack order.

While your Cavachon is still growing, on average, they can hold it approximately one hour for every month of their age. This means that if your 3-month-old puppy has been happily snoozing for two to three hours, as soon as they wake up, they will need to go outside.

Some of the first indications or signs that your puppy needs to be taken outside to relieve themselves will be when you see them:

• Sniffing around
• Circling
• Looking for the door

- Whining, crying, or barking
- Acting agitated

During the early stages of potty training, adding treats as an extra incentive can be a good way to reinforce how happy you are that your puppy is learning to relieve themselves in the right place. Slowly, treats can be removed and replaced with your happy praise, or you can give your puppy a treat after they are back inside.

Next, now that you have a new puppy in your life, you will want to be flexible with respect to adapting your schedule to meet their internal clocks to quickly teach your Cavachon puppy their new bathroom routine.

This means not leaving your puppy alone for endless hours at a time, because firstly, they are pack animals that need companionship and your direction at all times, plus long periods alone will result in the disruption of the potty training schedule you have worked hard to establish.

If you have no choice but to leave your puppy alone for many hours, make sure that you place them in a paper-lined room or pen where they can relieve themselves without destroying your newly-installed hardwood or favorite carpet. Remember, your Cavachon is a growing puppy with a bladder and bowels that they do not yet have complete control over.

Bell Training

A very easy way to introduce your new Cavachon puppy to house training is to begin by teaching them how to ring a bell whenever they need to go outside. A further benefit of training your puppy to ring a bell is that you will not have to listen to your puppy or dog whining, barking, or howling to be let out, and your door will not become scratched up from their nails.

Attach several bells to a piece of ribbon or string and hang it from a door handle, or tape it to a doorsill near the door where you will be taking your puppy out when they need to relieve themselves. The string will need to be long enough so that your puppy can easily reach the bell with their nose or a paw.

Next, each time you take your puppy out to relieve themselves, say the word 'out', and use their paw or their nose to ring the bell. Praise them for this 'trick' and immediately take them outside. This type of an alert system is an easy way to eliminate accidents in the home.

Melanie McCarthy of Cavachons From The Monarchy: "Personally I think bell training should be started after your dog is potty trained, to go outside. Bell training introduced too soon, is too overwhelming for a pup just learning 'where to eliminate'. Too many steps to learn at one time. Wait until the basic potty training is completely successful."

Kennel Training

When you train your Cavachon puppy to accept sleeping in their own kennel at nighttime, this will also help to accelerate their potty training. Because no puppy or dog wants to relieve themselves where they sleep, they will hold their bladder and bowels as long as they possibly can.

Presenting them with familiar scents by taking them to the same spot in the yard or the same street corner will help to remind and encourage them that they are outside to relieve themselves.

Use a voice cue to remind your puppy why they are outside, such as 'go pee', and always remember to praise them every time they relieve themselves in the right place, so that they quickly understand what you expect of them.

Exercise Pen Training

The exercise pen is a transition from kennel-only training and will be helpful for those times when you may have to leave your Cavachon puppy for more hours than they can reasonably be expected to hold it, although we repeat that many of our breeders don't think any dog should be left for more than four hours at a stretch.

Exercise pens are usually constructed of wire sections that you can  put together in whatever shape you desire, and the pen needs to be large enough to hold your puppy's kennel in one half of the pen, while the other half will be lined with newspapers, pee pads, or a potty pan with pellets.

Place your Cavachon puppy's food and water dishes next to the kennel and leave the kennel door open (or take it off), so they can wander in and out whenever they wish to eat or drink or go to the papers, pan, or pee pads if they need to relieve themselves.

Because they are already used to sleeping inside their kennel, they will not want to relieve themselves inside the area where they sleep. Therefore, your puppy will naturally go to the other half of the pen to relieve themselves.

Accelerated Potty Training

Thank you to Melanie McCarthy of Cavachons From The Monarchy who has produced, especially for us, her detailed guide to house training your Cavachon:

"This is what we recommend for the first four weeks of potty training; after that this needs to be continued but the owner can now give them more freedom. And what I describe below has to be interspersed with exercise and play time of a good intensity – at least every few hours. If puppies do not get this freedom to expend their puppy/high energy, they will at the end of the day be prone to aggressive behavior, including biting and nipping to try and get their energy out! This develops into a dangerous pattern. As a matter of fact, during training we do wake up the puppies and do not let them nap any longer than 45 minutes at a time – this will help the puppy expend that pent-up energy all day long.

1. Upon wake up, about 5:30 a.m., even before humans use the bathroom, take your puppy out of the closed crate, scooping him up quickly and taking a leash with you. Once he hears you walking about, he will have to 'go'. Go to designated outdoor spot and use the same spot for the next few weeks. Put the leash on (we use a leash with a loop at the end because at this age, the puppy gets his skin irritated with a regular collar and is very distracted by this.) When you come back in, set the alarm for an hourly schedule. Everything is from the perspective of planning for this hour.

2. Day one will be different than all other days. Please do not use any command when you get outside. Instead, put the puppy down on the ground and wait. He will eliminate. As he is eliminating say the command: "go potty" (this is what we use, it should be a short command).

3. Continue this method all day for the first day. If you do not do it this way, your puppy will have no idea what any command means. You have to say the command while you 'catch him' eliminating. Do this many times. Immediately 'mark' the behavior with a praise phrase and give a sliver of a treat simultaneously. No treats in the house, just for potty training. Exceptions are chew treats, veggies, fruits, nothing with caloric content.

4. Day two, you can start giving the command prior to his eliminating.

5. So after the wake-up trip outside, if your puppy does nothing, back in the crate for 10 minutes (door closed), then outside again. Keep repeating this every 10 minutes until he goes.

6. If you puppy does both urine and bowel movement, and after the treat reward and praise - which must be instantaneous - bring him in. He is again rewarded with complete freedom for 10 minutes. After 10 minutes, he is still rewarded with 'limited freedom' for another 10 – 15 minutes inside the exercise pen. If your puppy only does one – either urine or bowel movement but not both, bring him in and he goes straight to the exercise pen only for 10 minutes. He does not get complete freedom, he gets limited freedom. During

these freedom and limited freedom times, you will want to, several times a day, get into the pen and play very actively with him, interact with toys as well.

7. After this 'reward' time, puppy goes back into the crate, door shut. He stays in crate until that specific hour is up, unless it is breakfast, lunch or dinner time. Then you start the whole process again.

8. For purposes of potty training, instead of putting him back in the crate for the whole hour, you can hold your puppy as long as you want. You can also let him play outside during this time. Puppies will not eliminate while being held; puppies will eliminate while playing outside but that is ok. This will help you to help the puppy stay awake and expend more of that puppy energy.

9. If it is the first 'take out' trip for the day, after your pup has eliminated and while still in the pen, feed him breakfast. Give him 10 minutes to eat, remove food. Put him back in the crate after he takes his last bite, have him stay in the crate and after 10 minutes, start the potty routine again. After your puppy eats is one of those times that you must take him out again because digestion has started and moves along quickly; he will have to go again about 10 minutes after eating.

10. So the times that you start the 'go potty' trip outside are:

- First thing in the morning
- 10 minutes after each meal
- Immediately upon wake up from a nap (and we do not let them sleep for very long periods as you will have a puppy who has been crated too many hours during the day and will have anxiety at the end of the day)
- Last thing at the end of the day, as late as possible: 10 p.m. or 11 p.m.
- For the first two weeks, every 4 hours at night or if the puppy cries in the crate
- Keep the hourly schedule for the most part

11. At the four week mark, you can start expanding the freedom and limited freedom times. You will learn what is best for your puppy.

This method has some 'secret' tips that are critical. For example, on day one, it's best not to give any command outside to potty. The pup will have no idea what the person is talking about. Bring puppy out first thing in the morning and just WAIT. Once the puppy starts a bowel movement or starts to urinate, say the command, whatever it is. We say "go potty".

Do this for all of day one. If you don't, he won't make the connection very quickly, it will be much slower; I truly believe our pups are 85% of the way after 2 weeks. Even on the third day they have made the connection between the command and what we want from it.

Families who follow this training schedule report zero accidents in the house or very few, which they always attribute to their own mistakes. This method works and if you can put in the initial time, you won't have to worry about struggling with potty training for months and months."

We also find that our Cavachons never cry in the middle of the night unless they truly have to pee or poop. And this is usually limited to the first two weeks; when they whine at 2 a.m. you can be sure it is because they have to go potty.

Other puppies who cry in the middle of the night for other reasons may not yet be confident about the whole training system. The first two weeks we make a point of taking them out about 2 a.m.; then after that, there will be no need. Occasionally they will whine in the middle of the night and definitely have to go – depending upon whether their bladder and intestines were emptied out by 10 p.m. or not and how late they ate or drank.

Marking Territory

Both male and female dogs with intact reproductive systems mark territory by urinating. This is most often an outdoor behavior, but can happen inside if the dog is upset. Again, use an enzymatic cleaner to remove the odor and minimize the attractiveness of the location to the dog. Territory marking is especially prevalent in intact males. The obvious long-term solution is to have the dog neutered.

Marking territory is not a consequence of poor house training. The behavior can be seen in dogs that would otherwise never 'go' in the house. It stems from completely different urges and reactions.

Photo Credit: Victoria Johnson of Cosmic Cavachons & Cavapoos.

Dealing with Separation Anxiety

Separation anxiety manifests in a variety of ways, ranging from vocalizations to nervous chewing. Dogs that are otherwise well trained may urinate or defecate in the house. These behaviors begin when your dog recognizes **signs that you are leaving**. Triggers include picking up a set of car keys or putting on a coat. The dog may start to follow you around the house trying to get your attention, jumping up on you or otherwise trying to touch you.

It is imperative that you understand when you take on a Cavachon that **they are companion dogs**. They must have time to connect and be with their humans. You are the center of your dog's world. The behavior that a dog exhibits when it has separation anxiety is not a case of the animal being 'bad'. The poor thing experiences real distress and loneliness.

Being with him most of the time can cause him to be over-reliant on you, and then he will get stressed when left alone. As discussed earlier, it is wise to leave him on his own for a few minutes every day so he understands this is normal. You can increase this time gradually.

Remember that to a new puppy, you have now **taken the place of his mother and littermates**. He is completely reliant on you, so it is natural for him to follow you everywhere initially.

As well as puppies, you may also see separation anxiety in rescued dogs and senior (older) dogs.

13 Tips for Leaving Your Cavachon During the Daytime

Your Cavachon loves to be with you and they are very much in tune to recognizing those situations where you are going to leave them. They will go through a myriad of antics to avoid being left alone.

Being realistic, most of us have to go to work. While we recommend you take a couple of weeks off when you get your new puppy, the time will come to go back to work during the day.

1. Get a neighbor or friend to come in around lunchtime to spend some time with your Cavachon.

2. Employ a dog walker or come home yourself during your lunch break and take him for a walk.

3. Is there anyone, family, friends, etc. you could leave him with?

4. Exercise generates serotonin in the brain and has a calming effect. Walk him before your work and he will be less anxious and more ready for a good nap.

5. Leave some toys lying around for playtime to prevent boredom and destructive behaviors such as chewing and barking. Many toys can be filled with tasty treats that should do the trick!

6. Make sure that the temperature is moderate. You don't want your dog getting too cold or too hot in the place where you leave him.

7. Don't leave food down all day — he may become a fussy eater. Set specific meal times and remove it after 15-20 minutes if uneaten. This doesn't apply to water — make sure he has access to water at all times.

8. Leave him where he feels most comfortable. Near his crate with the door open is a good option.

9. Play some soothing music on repeat. There are dog-specific audio tracks that claim to ease separation anxiety. Often a dog will become concerned in a totally quiet environment and that may amplify their anxiety.

10. Stick to the same routine each day. Don't overly fuss him before you leave OR when you return. Keep it low key and normal.

11. Do your leaving routine such as putting shoes on, getting car keys, etc. and go out and come back almost immediately to build this experience into their brain gradually. Steadily increase the length over time. Do this almost as soon as your puppy comes home, so it won't be such a shock to him when you really do need to leave him alone.

12. Make sure other family members do things with your Cavachon, e.g. feeding, walking, playing, so he doesn't become over reliant on you.

13. Never punish him. They may do some bad things but this is not their fault and they do not mean to be bad on purpose. You WILL make the situation even worse if you do this.

Chapter 7 – Food & Exercise

This is perhaps the most **important chapter** in the book because whatever you feed your Cavachon affects the length and quality of his life. Remember too that they are driven by food, so will eat pretty much anything put in front of them, and they will eat as much as they can, so it is down to you as to what type of food they eat and how much.

Barby Wolfish of Pet Pointe: "I have heard people say their Cavachons are very picky eaters. Again, we did not find that to be the case, but we did not give in to her not wanting to eat her meal. As a pet store owner I see so many people that either give in and keep switching foods, or start feeding their dog pieces of chicken, cheese, etc to get them to eat. While many of these people foods are harmless, it may very well create a picky dog, one who holds out eating until something better is offered.

Also a number of Cavachon owners complain about tear staining (as a result of excessive tear production). My dog doesn't have this, but she is raw fed and you don't see that too often with raw fed dogs. Other owners have said what has helped is stainless steel bowls, filtered water, plain unsweetened yogurt and blueberries added to their diet."

When it comes to what food to serve to your precious Cavachon, the choices seem endless. There is **no one best food** because some dogs need higher fat and protein than others, while some prefer canned over dry.

Bear in mind that food manufacturers are out to maximize their profits, although as a rule you usually get what you pay for, so a more expensive food is generally more likely to provide **better nutrition** for your Cavachon in terms of minerals, nutrients, and higher quality meats in comparison to a cheap one, which will most likely **contain a lot of grain**.

Even today, far too many dog food choices continue to have far more to do with being convenient for us humans to serve than they do with being a well-balanced, healthy food choice.

We will help guide you through the maze of the supermarket shelves, but in order to choose the right food for your Cavachon, first it's important to understand a little bit about canine physiology and what Mother Nature intended when she created our furry companions. While humans are omnivores who can derive energy from eating plants, our canine companions are **natural carnivores**, which means they derive their energy and nutrient requirements from eating a diet consisting mainly or exclusively of the flesh of animals, birds, or fish — this provides proteins. Yes, proteins can be obtained from non-meat sources, but these are generally harder for the body to digest and have a higher chance of causing dietary intolerances.

Although dogs **can survive on an omnivorous diet**, this does not mean it is the best diet for them. Unlike humans, who are equipped with wide, flat molars for grinding grains, vegetables, and other plant-based materials, canine teeth are all pointed because they are designed to rip, shred, and tear into meat and bone.

Another obvious consideration when choosing an appropriate food source for our furry friends is the fact that dogs are born equipped with powerful jaws and neck muscles for the specific purpose of being able to pull down and tear apart their hunted prey.

The structure of the jaw of every canine is such that it opens widely to hold large pieces of meat and bone, while the mechanics of a dog's jaw permits only vertical (up and down) movement that is designed for crushing.

The Canine Digestive Tract

A dog's digestive tract is short and simple and designed to move their natural choice of food (hide, meat, and bone) quickly through their system. Given the choice, most dogs would never choose to eat plants and grains, or vegetables and fruits over meat, however, we humans continue to feed them a kibble-based diet that contains high amounts of vegetables, fruits, and grains with low amounts of meat. Part of this is because we've been taught that it's a healthy, balanced diet for humans, and therefore, we believe that it must be the same for our dogs, and part of this is because all the fillers that make up our dog's food are less expensive and easier to process than meat. While dogs can eat omnivorous foods, we are simply suggesting the **majority** of their diet should consist of meats.

Whatever you decide to feed your dog, keep in mind that just as too much wheat, other grains, and fillers in our human diet is having a detrimental effect on our health, the same can be very true for our best fur friends.

Our dogs are also suffering from many of the same life-threatening diseases that are rampant in our **human society**, as a direct result of consuming a diet high in genetically altered, impure, processed, and packaged foods.

Photo Credit: Jenna Lovatt of Pawfect Cavachons.

Top Feeding Tips

High-quality dog foods provide all the nutrients, vitamins, minerals, and calories that your dog needs. This makes it a lot easier than our human diet where we have to make sure we eat many varieties of foods, and even then, we may be deficient in an important mineral or vitamin. But a word of warning: just because a food is branded as premium **doesn't mean it is**. Essentially the word is meaningless marketing.

Before buying any dog food, read the label. The first (main ingredient by weight) listed ingredients **should be a meat** such as beef, chicken, lamb, **or fish**.

Foods with large amounts of fillers like cornmeal or meat by-products have a **low nutritional value**. They fill your dog up, but don't give him the necessary range of vitamins and minerals, and they increase daily waste produced.

If grains are used, look for **whole grains** (i.e., whole grain corn, whole grain barley) and not cheaper by-products (corn gluten meal, soybean meal).

High-end premium diets avoid grains altogether in favor of carbohydrates such as white or sweet potato.

Avoid artificial colors like Erythrosine, also known as Red No. 3, preservatives such as BHA, BHT, Ethoxyquin, and sweeteners such as sucrose or high fructose corn syrup. Cut out sugars and salt.

AAFCO stands for the Association of American Feed Control Officials. They develop guidelines for the production, labeling, and sale of animal foods. Choose a diet that complies with AAFCO specifications and conducts feeding trials. The label will say: Animal feeding tests using AAFCO procedures substantiate that (name of product) provides complete and balanced nutrition.

Grain free (or raw) is often recommended for the Cavachon. Many are **allergic** to corn, wheat, and some other grains. In addition, no soy should be in the dog food – it irritates them!

Wet foods are not appropriate for most growing dogs. They do not offer a good nutritional balance, and they are often upsetting to the stomach. Additionally, it's much harder to control portions with wet food, leading to young dogs being over or under fed.

Controlling portions is important. Give your dog the amount stipulated on the food packaging for his weight and age, and nothing more. If your Cavachon does not eat all of its meal in one go, you may be offering it too much. Many owners ask how many times a day they should feed and the reality is it doesn't matter — what does is the correct feeding amount. You then divide this up by the number of meals you wish to serve. Most owners opt for twice a day for adult dogs.

Stools should be firm, dark brown, and crinkly if portions are correct — if firm but softer towards the end, this is an indication of overfeeding. Stools are a **great indicator** of digestive upsets, so if you notice they are runny or hard, then there is a problem, as is excessive wind or an abnormal amount of feces. These should also not be brightly colored or smelly. Mucous in the stool is a common symptom of irritable bowel syndrome (IBS).

Invest in weighted food and water bowls made out of **stainless steel**. The weights prevent the mess of 'tip overs', and the material is much easier to clean than plastic. It does not hold odors or harbor bacteria.

Bowls in a stand that create an **elevated feeding surface** are also a good idea. Make sure your young dog can reach the food and water. Stainless steel bowl sets retail for less than $25 / £14.87.

Leave your Cavachon **alone** while it is eating from its bowl. Don't take the bowl away while he is eating. This causes anxiety, which can lead to **food aggression**.

Do you have more than one dog? I advise **feeding them separately** to completely avoid potential issues. One might try protecting his own food aggressively or try to eat the food designated for the other dog.

Feeding Your Puppy

As Cavachons age, they thrive on a graduated program of nutrition. Up to the age of four months, puppies should get **four small meals** a day. From age 4-8 months, **three meals** per day are appropriate. From 8 months on, feed your Cavachon **twice** a day and consider switching to an adult formula.

TIP - From the very beginning of weaning I put my hands into the puppies' bowls and feed them from my hands. I will take the food bowl from them and immediately offer them a tasty treat, then return their bowl. All of this teaches the puppy it is okay for hands to be around their food. I feel this is a very important life lesson where children are involved. Also, if a puppy grabs something that is not safe for them, they are much more willing to relinquish it.

Cavachons will eat pretty much anything and everything put in front of them, so it is up to you to control their portions!

Begin feeding your puppy by putting the food down for 10-20 minutes. If the dog doesn't eat, or only eats part of the serving, still **take the bowl up**. Don't give the dog more until the next feeding time. Scheduled feedings in measured amounts are the preferred option and are less likely to lead to a fussy eater.

To give your puppy a good start in life, rely on high-quality, premium dry puppy food. If possible, replicate the puppy's existing diet. A sudden **dietary switch** can cause gastrointestinal upset as puppies have sensitive stomachs. Take your pup to the vet if he has diarrhea or he has been vomiting for 48 hours or more.

Maintain the dog's existing routine if practical. To make an effective food transition, mix the existing diet with the new food, slowly changing the percentage of new to old over a period of 10 days.

Some breeders recommend not using puppy food. It can be high in protein and actually can cause the puppy to **grow too fast**, thus possibly creating bone growth issues. You may want to switch to a junior or adult food once he leaves puppyhood. Your vet will help decide when best to switch.

I highly recommend feeding puppies and dogs in the crate/kennel.

Adult Nutrition

The same basic nutritional guidelines apply to adult Cavachons. Always start with a high-quality, premium food. If possible, stay in the same product line the puppy received at the breeder. Graduated product lines help owners to create feeding programs that ensure nutritional consistency. This approach allows you to transition your Cavachon away from puppy food to an adult mixture, and in time, to a senior formula. This removes the guesswork from nutritional management.

Cavachons should be fed **at least** twice a day to avoid bloat, which can be fatal. You should also **avoid exercise** immediately before or after eating.

Say No to Table Scraps!

Dogs don't make it easy to say no when they beg at the table. If you let a Cavachon puppy have so much as that first bite, you've created a little monster – and one with an unhealthy habit.

Table scraps contribute to weight problems, and many human foods are toxic to dogs. They may be too rich for your Cavachon and cause him to scratch.

Never Feed These to Your Cavachon

Dangerous (some potentially fatal) items include:

- Chocolate
- Raisins and grapes
- Alcohol
- Human vitamins (especially those with iron)
- Mushrooms
- Garlic
- Onions
- Walnuts
- Macadamia nuts

Avoid sausages, sausage meat, and cooked manufactured meats as they can contain sulphite preservatives that can be harmful.

Never feed your Cavachon **cooked bones** as these can splinter and cause internal damage or become an intestinal obstruction. If you give your puppy a bone, watch him. Use only bones that are too large to choke on and take the item away at the first sign of splintering. Commercial chew toys rated 'puppy safe' are a much better option.

Never feed your dog from the table or your plate, as this encourages drooling and negative attention-seeking behaviors such as begging and barking.

The Dehydrated Diet (Freeze-Dried)

Dehydrated dog food comes in both raw and cooked forms, and these foods are usually air-dried to reduce moisture to the level where bacterial growth is inhibited.

The appearance of dehydrated dog food is very similar to dry kibble, and the typical feeding methods include adding warm water before serving, which makes this type of diet both healthy for our dogs and convenient for us to serve.

Dehydrated recipes are made from minimally-processed fresh whole foods to create a healthy and nutritionally-balanced meal that will meet or exceed the dietary requirements for healthy canines.

Dehydrating removes only the moisture from the fresh ingredients, which usually means that because the food has not already been cooked at a high temperature, more of the overall nutrition is retained.

A dehydrated diet is a convenient way to feed your dog a nutritious diet, because all you have to do is add warm water and wait five minutes while the food rehydrates so your Cavachon can enjoy a warm meal.

There are, however, some potential disadvantages. It is **more expensive** than other diets (you are paying for the convenience factor), and because of the processing can also **contain more preservatives** than you might ideally want.

Kibble Diet or Canned Food?

While many canine guardians are starting to take a closer look at the food choices they are making for their furry companions, there is no mistaking that the convenience and relative economy of dry dog food kibble, which had its beginnings in the 1940s, continues to make it the most popular dog food choice for most humans. It is basically one of the least expensive choices and is quick, easy, and convenient to serve.

Dry kibble dog food is less messy than canned, easier to measure, and can sit out all day without going bad. It is more economical per pound and is more energy-dense than canned food. This is because dry food is usually only 10% water, compared with about 75% water in cans. It takes a much larger volume of canned food to supply the nutrients your dog needs, as a can effectively only has 25% food. You are also likely to have to put half-finished cans in your fridge to keep them from going off, and they cause a strong smell which is unpleasant to some.

Be wary of cheap kibble, which often has high grain content and **is a false economy** as they have to eat a lot to be well-nourished.

Canned-food diets do have some **advantages**. Food manufacturers artificially boost the taste appeal of dry kibble by coating it with tempting fats, gravy, and other flavorings. In comparison, the wet and moist food fresh out of a can is much more edible to your Cavachon and often contains more protein, fat, and less additives and preservatives. The texture and smell also have added appeal to their senses!

The BARF/Raw Diet

Raw feeding advocates believe that the ideal diet for their dog is one that would be very similar to what a dog living in the wild would have access to, and these canine guardians are often opposed to feeding their dog any sort of commercially manufactured pet foods.

On the other hand, those opposed to feeding their dogs a raw or Biologically Appropriate Raw Food (BARF) diet believe that the risks associated with food-borne illnesses during the handling and feeding of raw meats outweigh the purported benefits.

A typical BARF diet is made up of 60-80% of raw meaty bones (RMB). This is bones with about 50% meat, (e.g. chicken neck, back, and wings) and 20-40% of fruit and vegetables, offal, meat, eggs, or dairy foods.

Many owners directly oversee the raw diets, which usually consist of raw meat and bones, with some vegetables, fruits, supplements, and added grains.

Alternatively, you can buy commercial raw diet meals, which come either fresh or frozen. These supply all of the dog's requirements and are usually in a meat patty form.

Many owners and breeders agree that their dogs thrive on a raw or BARF diet and strongly believe that the potential benefits of feeding a dog a raw food diet are many, including:

- Healthy, shiny coats
- Decreased shedding
- Fewer allergy problems
- Healthier skin
- Cleaner teeth
- Fresher breath
- Higher energy levels
- Improved digestion
- Smaller stools
- Strengthened immune system
- Increased mobility in arthritic pets

- General increase or improvement in overall health
- Ability to control what is in your Cavachon's food bowl
- Ability to avoid ingredients they are allergic or intolerant to
- No preservatives or additives

All dogs, whether working breed or lap dogs, are amazing athletes in their own right, therefore every dog deserves to be fed the best food available. A raw diet is a direct evolution of what dogs ate before they became our domesticated pets and we turned toward commercially prepared, easy-to-serve dry dog food that required no special storage or preparation.

This all sounds good doesn't it? So what **are the downsides**?

- Can be time consuming — less convenient.
- More expensive than other diets.
- Diet may not be balanced unless you are very careful — your Cavachon may become deficient in minerals and vitamins.
- Raw vegetables are often poorly digested by dogs.
- Safety for the elderly and young children — raw diets have been found to contain Salmonella, Campylobacter, E. coli, Clostridium perfringens, Clostridium botulinium, and Staphylococcus aureus. These are all known human and canine pathogens.
- Safety to your Cavachon — some raw foods contain pathogens which can make your dog very sick (even fatally) such as Neospora caninum, found in raw beef, Nanophyetus salmincola, found in raw salmon, and Trichinella spiralis, found in raw pork.

Food Allergies

Unfortunately, just like humans, Cavachons sometimes react badly to certain foods. It is important to look out for signs, especially **itchy skin**, but also rubbing of the face on the floor or carpet, excessive scratching, ear infections, hot patches and rash on the chin and face.

The **most common allergies** are to beef, dairy products, chicken, wheat, eggs, corn, and soy.

How Much to Feed?

There is no definite answer because it depends on a number of varying factors. Your Cavachon is unique. Even with two the same age, they can have differing metabolic levels, with one being very energetic compared to the other, which might be a slouch!

The amount of daily exercise you are able to give your Cavachon is a critical factor because they will burn off more calories the more they do and thus need to eat more without putting on weight.

As a general rule, smaller Cavachons have faster metabolisms so require a higher amount of food per pound of body weight. Younger Cavachons also need more food than seniors, who by that age have a slower metabolic rate.

The type of food you serve is also a factor. There are definitely some lesser quality (low priced) foods that may have the weight (bulk) but offer less in terms of nutrition and goodness.

Be slightly cynical when reading the recommended daily allowance on the labels because they are usually higher than need be. Remember this is from the manufacturer who profits the more your Cavachon eats!

Obesity is now a real problem for many dogs because their owners are unaware that they are overweight. Lethargy, high blood pressure, joint problems, heart problems, and diabetes are all much more common in overweight dogs.

Treats

Treats are a great way to reward your Cavachon for good behavior and also for training purposes, however there are some cautions to note. Many treats are high in sugar and can contain artificial additives, milk, and fat.

Good quality treats can have nutritional value, but you really don't want to overuse them; I suggest they make up a maximum of 15% of their total daily calorie intake. Try to use **praise as a reward** instead, so you are not always using treats every time he needs rewarding.

Don't forget that treats don't just come out of a packet or box, they can also include normal items such as steamed vegetables, apple slices, and carrot sticks.

A great way to reward and stimulate your Cavachon is a toy that dispenses the treat (food) when he works a puzzle out. The best-known is perhaps the Kong. This chew toy is made of nearly indestructible rubber. Kong sells specially shaped treats and different things you can squeeze inside, but you can stuff it with whatever he likes best.

Nina Ottosson is a genius Swedish pioneer in the world of interactive dog puzzle toys. Her offerings come in a variety of levels of difficulty and in both plastic and wood.

TIP - Take a hot dog, cut it into 4ths along its length and then chop the long, skinny lengths into lots of little pieces. Cook in the microwave for at least 2 minutes longer than you would normally cook a hot dog. You will have 50+ pieces to use as rewards.

Ingredients — Be Careful!

Learning to understand the labels on the back of packaging is really important to understand the quality of food you are giving to your beloved Cavachon.

Some manufacturers can use 'cute' tricks to **disguise** the amount of grains in their product. They list them separately (to push them down the list order) but added together they can add up to a sizeable amount. The reverse is true, where they add all the meat ingredients together as one so it appears as the first listed ingredient — but check what else the food consists of!

Although milk contains several beneficial nutrients, it also contains a high proportion of the sugar lactose. As in humans, many dogs have **real difficulties digesting** lactose and as a result, milk products can bring on stomach pains, flatulence, diarrhea, and even vomiting.

When you see meat listed, this refers to the clean flesh of slaughtered animals (chicken, cattle, lamb, turkey, etc.). The flesh can include striated skeletal muscle, tongue, diaphragm, heart, esophagus, overlying fat and the skin, sinew, nerves, and blood vessels normally found with that flesh.

When you see meat by-products listed, this refers to the clean parts of slaughtered animals, not including meat. These include lungs, spleen, kidneys, brain, liver, blood, bone, some fatty tissue, and stomach and intestines freed of their contents (it doesn't include hair, horns, teeth, or hooves).

Don't mistake dry food as being very low in meat content compared to a wet food that lists fresh meat as an ingredient. Fresh meat consists of two-thirds water, so you need to discount the water when doing your comparisons between the two.

The **Guaranteed Analysis** on the label is very helpful, as it contains the exact percentages of crude protein, fat, fiber, and moisture.

Don't be scared off if the main ingredient is chicken meal rather than fresh beef. This is simply chicken that is dehydrated, and it contains more protein than fresh chicken, which is 80 percent water. The same is true for beef, fish, and lamb.

Feeding Older Cavachons

We have a whole chapter on looking after your aging Cavachon, but while we are here, we will make some observations on feeding.

Once your Cavachon passes the age of 8, he can be considered a 'senior', and his body has different requirements to those of a young dog — you may notice signs of your dog slowing down, putting on weight, or having joint issues. This is the time to discuss and involve your vet in considering switching to a senior diet.

Because his body's metabolism is slowing down, the adult diet he is on may have too many calories that **cannot be burned off** with the amount of exercise he is capable of. This isn't your fault, so don't feel guilty.

Don't let the pounds pile on. They are much harder to take off than put on, and his weight **literally affects his longevity** as more strain is being put on his internal organs and joints. A senior diet is specially formulated to have a lower calorie count. They tend to be higher in fiber to prevent constipation, which senior dogs can be prone to.

Some breeders suggest supplements such as glucosamine and chondroitin, which assist joints.

The opposite problem is loss of appetite. It may be as simple as needing a change of food, but it could be issues with his teeth. A more moist food may help, but first get his teeth checked by your vet.

A breeder friend of mine told me of his aging dogs barking for no apparent reason. He started feeding them Pro Plan Bright Minds and saw a difference for the better within a few weeks. He says they are more alert and the barking for no reason just stopped.

What the Breeders Advise on Feeding and Diet

Jenna Lovatt of Pawfect Cavachons: "Diet is very important for all dogs. I wean my puppies on a natural holistic kibble called Eden, which consists of an 80/20 diet. It is 80% meat and 20% fruit and veg. They produce only the best foods possible that are 100% natural. They openly list all ingredients and they are the first British food to be rated 5 out of 5 stars on 'The All About Dog Food' website. All my dogs and puppies thrive on this kibble and have gorgeous glossy coats."

Linda Kaiser of Smooch My Pups: "I feed my lactating moms and my puppies exclusively a raw diet. My moms are very well hydrated by this diet, unlike a dry kibble that dehydrates them, and therefore (they) produce an abundance of nutritional milk for the babies to grow up on. The puppies are extremely healthy and robust! When it comes time for the puppies to start eating solid food, there is an easy transition. This diet not only proves to radiate from the inside out, by way of their shiny thick healthy coats, but also maintains healthy organs and it prevents periodontal disease. If you can't feed your dog a raw diet, for whatever reason, please think enough of him/her to at least feed a topical enzyme/probiotic so they can process their food better. I choose to feed them what they were designed to eat and encourage all of my families to do the same. I have the most invested. If a dog develops something wrong, the first person that is pointed to is the breeder. Please love your dog enough to feed the best you can buy. If you can't do raw, then do a canned food that doesn't have a lot of carbohydrates or sugars in it. I feed Nature's Variety Instinct Raw Beef or Lamb and add raw venison when I can."

Nichola Lack of Cracking Cavachons: "A good quality food is very important. Many opt for the 80/20 mix foods if feeding commercial dog food. There is also the option of raw feeding. Many are scared to do this but it is very safe if done correctly. There are many Facebook groups to help advise on raw feeding and I would highly recommend learning about it before jumping in and getting it wrong."

Melanie McCarthy of Cavachons From The Monarchy: "We feed our puppies Orijen Puppy. We did extensive research before we settled on this food. It is a Canadian food and we found that Canada employs higher standards in its puppy diets than does the U.S."

Linda & Steve Rogers of Timshell Farm say: "Great natural treats – CARROTS. They serve to help keep their teeth clean and are much healthier for them than commercial biscuits, etc. The dogs LOVE them! Our grocery store sells 15 pound bags for $10. Economical, healthy treat!

"For upset stomachs with puppies – keep a can of pure pumpkin on hand – not the pie mix, but pure pumpkin. Give a tablespoon on top of dry food, once a day. Alternate this with a tablespoon of plain yogurt the next day. Great for stomach/digestive problems."

Managing Your Active Cavachon

Cavachons are medium-energy dogs, and although they certainly have the capacity to become lazy couch potatoes, they can also turn hyperactive and destructive if bored. They need regular exercise to stay in good health, physically and emotionally!

Your Cavachon likes routine, so establish one and stick to it as much as possible. Just because you have a garden or yard does not mean that you don't need to walk your dog. He needs mental stimulation as well as physical.

 When Cavachons are young, exercise should be limited in as much as pounding pavements should be avoided. I think it is imperative not to exercise puppies under 6 months. I have seen over-exercised baby puppies end up as adults with very unsound joints, as they have been taken for too many long walks. Young puppies have soft bones/joints like a child, and they don't really firm up until 5-6 months old. Over exercising can upset the growth plates that can cause weakness in the elbows, pasterns and stifles.

Free running for short bursts of a few minutes at a time is fine, and as the puppy reaches around six months the periods of free running can be increased.

Once muscles and bones are grown when the dog is around twelve months, really they can take as much exercise as the owner wants to give. This should be on a daily basis and not confined to weekends!

Cavachons are intelligent and need mental stimulation in addition to physical training, and may become fractious if their lifestyle is too sedentary.

Photo Credit: Bailey from Jen Sweetman.

As a rule of thumb, around **half an hour free running daily** will be enough to keep your Cavachon toned, and this coupled with a good-sized garden to patrol will keep him on his toes.

Collar or Harness?

Regardless of breed, I'm not a big fan of using a traditional collar. I wouldn't enjoy a choking sensation and assume my dog wouldn't either. That said, many breeders prefer collars. My current favorite on-body restraints are the harnesses that look like vests. They offer a point of attachment for the lead on the back between the shoulders.

This arrangement directs pressure away from the neck and allows for easy, free movement. Young dogs are less resistant to this system and don't strain against a harness the way they will with a collar.

It's best to take your Cavachons with you to the pet store to get a proper fit. Sizing for a dog is much more unpredictable than you might think. I have seen dogs as large as 14 lbs. / 6.35 kg take an 'Extra Small', depending on their build. Regardless of size, harnesses retail in a range of $20-$25 / £11.88-£14.85.

Standard Leash or Retractable?

The decision to buy a standard, fixed-length leash or a retractable lead is, for the most part, a matter of personal preference. Some facilities like groomers, vet clinics, and dog daycares ask that you not use a retractable lead on their premises. The long line represents a trip and fall hazard for other human clients.

Fixed-length leashes often sell for as little as $5 / £2.97, while retractable leads are less than $15 / £8.91.

Learning to respond to your control of the leash is an important behavioral lesson for your Cavachon. Do not **drag a dog** on a lead or **jerk him**. If he sits down and refuses to budge, pick him up. Don't let the dog be in charge of the walk or you'll have the devil's own time regaining the upper hand.

Cavachons are smart, active dogs. They'll associate the lead with adventures and time with you. Don't be at all surprised if your dog picks up words associated with excursions like 'go', 'out', 'car' or 'walk'.

Dog Walking Tips

Active dogs like Cavachons are 'into' the whole walking experience. This is an excellent opportunity to use the activity to build and reinforce good behaviors on command.

Photo Credit: Sophie from Robert Maxwell.

Teach your dog to sit by using the word and making a downward pointing motion with your finger or indicating the desired direction with the palm of your hand. Do not attach the lead until your dog complies, rewarding his patience with the words he most wants to hear: 'Okay, let's go!'

If your dog jerks or pulls on the leash, stop, pick up the dog, and start the walk over with the 'sit' command. Make it clear that the walk ceases when the dog misbehaves. Praise your dog for walking well on the end of the lead and for stopping when you stop. Reinforce positive behaviors during walks. Your dog will get the message and show the same traits during other activities.

The Importance of Basic Commands

It is to your advantage to go through a basic obedience class with your dog. By their nature, canines are eager to please, but they need direction. Much of this lies in a consistent routine and command 'language'.

Experts agree that most dogs can pick up between 165 and 200 words, but they can't extrapolate more than one meaning. If, for instance, your dog barks, you need to use the same command in response, like 'quiet'. If he picks something up, you might say 'drop it'.

For problem jumping, most owners go with 'off' or 'down'. The point is to pick a set of words and use them over and over to create a basic vocabulary for your dog. Both the word and your tone of voice should convey your authority and elicit the desired response.

 This is not a difficult process with a breed whose native intelligence is as advanced as that of the Cavachon. Investigate enrollment in an obedience class through your local dog club or ask your vet about trainers in your area. Start the lessons early in your dog's life by offering him the stability of consistent reactions.

Training should only be done for a few minutes. Make it positive. Remember, he won't learn if he is afraid, so make training fun and upbeat at all times! If you start being frustrated or upset, it is time to stop for the day. Several short training sessions work better than a long one. Using small treats really helps!

Teaching an emergency 'come' will help if your dog ever gets loose. To teach this, you need a fabulous treat, perhaps a few licks from a jar of baby food meat. Put your dog on a long lead (50 feet). Have someone hold the lead and engage your dog while you walk to the other end. Then call your dog's name and a one word signal in a very loud, excited voice. This call needs to be different from the one you use when you teach a normal come, such as 'here!' or 'now!'. When the dog comes, give him lots of praise and several licks from the jar of baby food. Do this many times and practice it weekly. If the time ever comes that your dog is loose or in danger, this emergency 'come' may save your dog's life!

Photo Credit: Sophie from Robert Maxwell.

Linda & Steve Rogers of Timshell Farm tell us just how intelligent the Cavachon is compared to other dog breeds: "Cavachons are bright and happy dogs and on a scale of 1 to 10, I'd give them an 8. Cavaliers are smarter than people think – they're just quiet about it. Bichons are intelligent, also but sometimes would rather focus on playing than learning!"

Play Time and Tricks

Always offer praise and show pleasure for correct responses. This makes training just another form of play – and **Cavachons love to play!**

The speed with which your dog will amass and destroy a collection of toys may shock you. Avoid soft rubber toys — they shred into small pieces, which the dog will swallow. Opt for rope toys instead or chew toys that can withstand the abuse. You can buy items made out of this tough material in the $1-$5 / £0.59-£2.97 range. Don't buy anything with a squeaker or any other part that presents a choking hazard.

Never give your dog rawhide or pig's ears, which soften and present a choking hazard. Also avoid cow hooves, which can splinter and puncture the cheek or palate.

Playtime is important, especially for a dog's natural desire to chase. Try channeling this instinct with toys and games. If a dog has no stimulation and has nothing to chase, they can start to chase their own tail, which can lead to problems. Dogs that don't get enough exercise are also more likely to develop problem behaviors like chewing, digging, and barking.

Toys can be used to simulate the dog's natural desire to hunt. For example, when they catch a toy, they will often shake it and bury their teeth into it, simulating the killing of their prey.

Allow your dog to fulfill **a natural desire** to chew. This comes from historically catching their prey and then chewing the carcass. Providing chews or bones can prevent your dog from destroying your home. Deer antlers are wonderful toys for a Cavachon; most love them. They do not smell, are all-natural, and do not stain or splinter. I recommend the antlers that are not split: they last longer.

Playing with your dog is not only a great way of getting them to use up their energy, but it is also a **great way of bonding** with them as they have fun. Dogs love to chase and catch balls, but make sure that the ball is too large to be swallowed.

I also recommend having a toy mobile over the pen with various soft and hard toys hanging down, also I have a game that you hide food under and they have to move the pieces to get the food ... great to make them use their senses. Puppies need to experience a variety of different textures, whether rubber or plastic soft fabrics.

Chapter 8 – Grooming

The Cavachon is a relatively **high-maintenance dog** in terms of grooming. As **soon as your Cavachon is home**, work on desensitizing him to your touch. This will help when you come to groom him and also when you have to visit the vets. Start slowly to begin with and build up the time as he seems comfortable. Touch areas such as his gums and nails so these areas can be maintained by you.

Photo Credit: Melanie McCarthy of Cavachons From The Monarchy

Don't allow yourself to get caught in the "my Cavachon doesn't like it" trap, which is an excuse many owners will use to avoid regular grooming sessions. **Do not allow** your dog to dictate whether they will permit a grooming session, as you are setting a dangerous precedent. In time, your Cavachon **will love** to be tickled, rubbed, and scratched in certain favorite places. This is why grooming is a great source of pleasure and a way to bond together.

Regular brushing helps your Cavachon in many ways. Aerating the coat ensures healthy growth by promoting good blood circulation. It helps to keep grease levels down which can block pores and cause sebaceous cysts. He will also **shed less hair** around your house.

If you don't brush (groom) them, their loose hairs become matted, forming heavy wads, which can cause skin complaints and soreness.

The Cavachon has a medium-length coat, like both of the parent breeds, and it can be quite thick and wavy. For this reason you need to brush your Cavachon several times a week and have him professionally groomed and trimmed on average every 5-6 weeks.

Melanie McCarthy of Cavachons From The Monarchy: "They should be professionally groomed at least every 5 weeks. Yes, some may like the hair longer, but then you begin to have matting and snarls and Cavachons, like Bichons, can develop hot spots on their skin, which erupt as painful lesions.

"Also, toenails need to be checked every 4 weeks; be sure they are not hitting the floor. One can gauge this by listening to the dog walk. You should not hear the nails touching the floor, they should be 'just off' the floor. This is important as it can change the gait of the dog and eventually cause knee or hip problems.

"Every week, the owner needs to trim hairs around the eyes so the corneas do not get scratched. Very importantly, clean around the eyes once a day to clean up excessive tearing and prevent tear staining. Yes, they are high maintenance dogs, but worth it!"

In terms of brushes, the standard options include:

- **Bristle** brushes, which work well with all coats from long to short. They remove dirt and debris and distribute natural oils throughout the coat.

- **Wire-pin** brushes, which are for medium to long coats and look like a series of pins stuck in a raised base.

- **Slicker** brushes are excellent for smoothing and detangling longer hair.

You can often find combination, two-headed brushes. They'll save you a little money and make your grooming sessions easier.

Each of these types of brush costs less than $15 / £9 and often less than $10 / £6.

Personally, I find the best grooming tool to use on your Cavachon at home is a wire pin brush – brush your Cavachon from head to toe, moving in the direction of hair growth. If you come across a matt or tangle, try to work through it with a wide-tooth comb. If you absolutely cannot get it out, you can cut it out. To do so, pinch the hair below the matt as close to your Cavachon's skin as you can – this will help to make sure you do not accidentally cut your dog's skin – then just cut the matt free.

Spraying the coat with a conditioner before combing will keep it shining and clean.

TIP: A friend of mine swears by the **Tangle Teezer** brush. Although it's for women's hair, it apparently works like a charm. She says brushing is now fun and relaxing because her dog believes he is getting a massage.

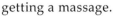

Grooming/brushing sessions are an excellent opportunity to examine your dog's skin to do a **quick health check**. Look for any growths, lumps, bumps, or wounds. Also have a good look at his ears, eyes, and mouth. Check between paw pads for any balls of matted fur, which can become hard with dirt and grease, causing pain.

While you can learn how to trim your Cavachon's coat yourself, it can be a challenging task that might be best left to the professionals. A professional groomer will know how to handle your Cavachon's thick coat and will be able to trim it according to your preferences.

There are several different kinds of cuts that you might choose to go with.

A puppy cut involves trimming the hair very close to the body, leaving it a little longer on the face and tail.

A show cut involves more shaping than trimming, adjusting the coat so it follows the contours of the dog's body.

A panda cut is halfway between the two – it is a little longer than a puppy cut but shorter than a show cut and it follows the contours of the Cavachon's body.

The type of cut you select is up to you but keep in mind that a puppy cut is easier to maintain. If you decide that you want to start grooming your Cavachon yourself, you can ask the groomer to show you how to do it.

Linda & Steve Rogers of Timshell Farm: "Some people like the longer look on their Cavachons and this requires daily (deep) grooming to keep mats and tangles. The longer look can mean longer time between groomings. The shorter cut ('puppy cut' or 'kennel cut') is so cute and keeps them clean and tangle/mat free (though you do still have to brush daily, it goes much quicker). To keep them in this short mode, grooming needs to be done a bit more frequently."

Nichola Lack of Cracking Cavachons: "I highly recommend brushing several times a week. I also advise a nice metal comb, to part the fur to make sure you groom all layers of fur. Simply brushing over the top will not remove any matts."

Owner Jen Sweetman, owner of Bailey: "For me brushing daily is a must to avoid matting. Cavachon's fur can differ greatly, but Bailey has more Bichon fur so can matt easily if not brushed often. Detangling brushes are great and also slicker brushes to give their fur that fluffy look. Getting them used to being bathed, brushed and blow dried from being a puppy is strongly advisable as Cavachons require regular visits to the groomers."

Eyes

Your Cavachon's eyes should be clear and bright, with no excessive discharge apart from that left over from sleeping.

Older dog's eyes may show signs of becoming cloudy; this could be a sign of cataracts, and if you are worried, then it is worth speaking to your vet.

You should wipe their eyes regularly with a warm, damp cloth to remove the buildup of secretions in the corners of the eyes. This can be both unattractive and uncomfortable for the dog as the hair becomes glued together.

If this build up is not removed every day, it can quickly become a cause of **bacterial yeast growth** that can lead to smelly eye infections.

Ears

Your Cavachon's ears should be frequently checked. Look for a dark discharge or regular scratching, as this can signal an infection. Affected ears also have a stronger smell than usual.

Cavachons that have a lot of hair growing inside the ear can struggle with infection, as the hair can prevent normal healthy wax leaving the ear area. The hair inside the ears needs to be cut with safety scissors (blunted end).

Ear mites can become a problem if your dog comes into contact with an infected animal. Too small to be seen by the naked eye, a bad ear mite infestation can cause the dog a lot of unrest and distress. Both infections and ear mites can be diagnosed and treated easily with drops, antibiotics, or both, as prescribed by your vet.

There are many ear cleaning creams, drops, oils, rinses, solutions, and wipes formulated for cleaning your dog's ears that you can purchase from your local pet store or veterinarian's office. You may prefer to use a home remedy that will just as efficiently clean your

Cavachon's ears, such as **Witch Hazel** or a 50:50 mixture of hydrogen peroxide and purified water.

Ear powders, which can be purchased at any pet store, are designed to help keep your Cavachon's ears dry while at the same time inhibiting the growth of bacteria that can lead to infections. You may want to apply a little ear powder after washing the inside of your dog's ears to help ensure that they are totally dry.

Bathing

For the most part, Cavachons are a clean breed so you shouldn't have to worry about bathing your dog too often, although most are perfectly happy to have baths, and even seem to enjoy the water. In fact, bathing your Cavachon too frequently could lead to dry skin and itching on top of this breed's natural risk for skin problems.

If you do need to bathe your Cavachon, give him a good brushing before you do. Fill your bathtub with a few inches of warm water then place your Cavachon in it.

Cavachons have low-hanging ears which puts them at an increased risk for ear infections. Because the ears hang down over the head, there is not a lot of air circulation under the ear – if the area gets wet it could become a breeding ground for bacteria. So remember **not to get your pet's head and ears wet**. Clean the dog's head and face with a warm, wet washcloth only. Rinse your dog's coat with a mixture of 1tbs shampoo and 2 cups water then pour over dog. Use clean, fresh water to remove all residue. Towel your pet dry and make sure he doesn't get chilled. The rinse is really the most important step of the whole procedure. If any shampoo is left in the coat, it will irritate the skin and lead to 'hot spots'.

TIP: Try using Chamois cloths to dry your Cavachon. They work well, and they don't have to be laundered as much. They just air dry and can be washed in the washing machine. However, DO NOT put the Chamois in the dryer. I have found that they work much better than towels.

DON'T make the mistake of using human shampoo or conditioner on your Cavachon, because they have a different pH balance than us and it will be too harshly acidic for their coat and skin, which can create skin problems. Always purchase a shampoo for your dog that is **specially formulated** to be gentle and moisturizing on your Cavachon's coat and skin, will not strip the natural oils, and will nourish your dog's coat to give it a healthy shine.

Nail Trimming

Coat maintenance is not the only grooming chore necessary to keep your Cavachon in good shape. Even dogs that walk on asphalt or other rough surfaces will need to have their nails trimmed from time to time. That said, if you do walk your Cavachon a lot they won't need as much trimming. If nails get too long they can split and get damaged more easily.

If your pet is agreeable, this is a job you can perform at home with a trimmer especially designed for use with dogs. I prefer those with plier grips. They're easier to handle and quite cost effective, selling for under $20 / £11.88.

Never use a regular Dremel™ tool, as it will be too high speed and will burn your dog's toenails. Only use a slow speed Dremel™, such as Model 7300-PT Pet Nail Grooming Tool (approx. $40/£20). You can also purchase the flexible hose attachment for the Dremel which is much easier to handle and can be held like a pencil.

Snip off the nail tips at a 45-degree angle at the point where the nail begins to curve at the tip, before the point where the pink area, referred to as the quick, is visible. Be careful not to cut too far down, otherwise you will hurt your Cavachon and cause heavy bleeding. If this happens, don't panic. Use a piece of cotton or tissue and hold pressure on it until it stops bleeding. Buy some **styptic powder** just in case. This antiseptic clotting agent causes the vessels to contract, thereby stemming the blood loss. Apply to the nail only, and a warning — initially it will sting your Cavachon.

If you are apprehensive about performing this chore, ask your vet tech or groomer to walk you through it the first time.

Melanie McCarthy of Cavachons From The Monarchy: "Viewing the toe nail photo, try to allow at least 2 millimeters of white area left on the nail before the pink area, where the vein is located. Black nails are often more difficult to see the quick, but by using the pad and straight area beneath the toe nail, you can gauge where the extra length of nail is at that needs to be trimmed. We prefer the scissor-type toe nail clippers over the guillotine type. Using the guillotine type can be painful to your dog.

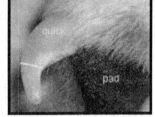

"After we use our scissor-type clippers on the toe nails we then use our grinder to smooth off or 'file down' the rough edges and to grind back the quick slightly. The grinder we use is a Dremel, with variable speeds and we use it at ¾ speed. This is a plug-in type which has much more power than the battery operated Dremels which are labelled for cutting the nails of dogs."

Anal Glands

All dogs can suffer from blocked anal glands. Many dogs express them every time they poop (the sacs/glands are around a dog's anus but occasionally the sacs fill with fluid and your Cavachon will need some help to release the fluid).

He may scoot or rub his bottom on the ground or carpet (you may also notice a foul odor). If this occurs, the glands will need expressing to prevent an abscess from forming. This is a sensitive task and one that a veterinarian or an experienced groomer should perform.

Barby Wolfish of Pet Pointe: "If your dog is fed a healthy diet this should not be a problem. My vet suggested adding a probiotic to my dog's diet after she had a problem with her anal glands at about 9 years of age, and she has not had a problem since."

Fleas and Ticks

I'm including fleas and ticks under grooming because that's when they're usually found. Don't think that if your Cavachon has 'passengers' you're doing something wrong, or that the dog is at fault. This is a part of dog ownership. Sooner or later, it will happen. Address the problem, but don't panic.

Do NOT use a commercial flea product on a puppy of less than 12 weeks of age, and be extremely careful with adult dogs. Most of the major products contain pyrethrum. The chemical causes long-term neurological damage and even fatalities in small dogs.

To get rid of fleas, bathe your dog in warm water with a standard canine shampoo. Comb the animal's fur with a fine-toothed flea comb, which will trap the live parasites. Submerge the comb in hot soapy water to kill the fleas.

Wash the dog's bedding and any soft materials with which he has come in contact. Look for any accumulations of flea dirt, which is blood excreted by adult fleas. Wash the bedding and other surfaces daily for at least a week to kill any remaining eggs before they hatch.

While nobody likes to use chemicals regarding their dogs, it seems almost impossible to use anything else in the battle with fleas, ticks and bugs! For the last decade or so I have used a safe lawn product in my dog yards that kill fleas, ticks, spiders, mosquitoes and more. I go by the directions and don't allow the dogs to go to those yards until after a rain or watering after application, since then I usually do not need to use any other products on the dogs. I do a lawn application the end of March, the end of June and the last one in September.

TIP - Nexgard is a treatment for fleas and it also treats for heartworms, so it is time efficient. Also, Dawn dish soap kills fleas and is safe for all ages.

If your Cavachon is outside a lot then check for ticks on a regular basis, as these eight-legged parasites can carry diseases. Look out for warning signs such as lack of movement, swollen joints, fever, and loss of appetite.

If you find a tick, coat it with a thick layer of petroleum jelly for 5 minutes to suffocate the parasite and cause its jaws to release. Pluck the tick off with a pair of tweezers using a straight motion.

An alternative is a tick remover which is a tool similar to a bottle opener. Never just jerk a tick off a dog. The parasite's head stays behind and continues to burrow into the skin, making a painful sore.

Clean the wound with antiseptic and make sure to clean your tweezers with isopropyl alcohol to sterilize them. Keep an eye on the area where the tick was to see if an infection surfaces. If the skin remains irritated or infected, make an appointment with your veterinarian.

Victoria Johnson of Cosmic Cavachons & Cavapoos says: "All my puppies are naturally raised. I prefer to avoid harsh chemicals and over-vaccination, choosing instead to use homeopathic nosodes, natural wormers and work on keeping their immune systems healthy. I feed a raw, species-appropriate diet and I don't treat my dogs for fleas unless I see them. If I ever do I will also look for a natural alternative, of which there are many.

I also do regular worm counts on my older dogs to see if they actually have worms. **Diotomaceous Earth** is one of my wormers of choice; added to the food daily it helps to keep your dog clear of worms but if purchasing, make sure it's food grade. For dogs that don't like extras added to their food, I use **Four Seasons**. Ground pumpkin seeds can also be used. There is a wealth of information on natural rearing and I believe it's the best way to keep your dog healthy."

Chapter 9 – Training and Problem Behaviors

Cavachons are fun, loving dogs and are generally easy to train. When it comes to dog training there are several different methods to choose from. For Cavachons, however, positive reinforcement training is the most effective. With this type of training you reward your dog for performing desired behaviors and, in doing so, reinforce that behavior. If your dog gets a treat for sitting when you tell him to sit, he will be more likely to repeat that behavior in the future.

Photo Credit: Hannah training Rosie by Corey Seeman.

Cavachons have an eager-to-please attitude which will help to speed up the process. The key to training your Cavachon effectively is to make things as simple as possible and to make sure that your dog understands what you want him to do. If you do not consistently reward your Cavachon for performing the desired behavior during the early stages of training, he may not learn which behavior it is that you want or he might become frustrated.

Introduce him to new sights, sounds, people, and places. Let him interact with other dogs in a controlled environment. There, the dog is safe to deal with fear and timidity without blustering self-defense postures. You'll get a better-mannered dog and a greater understanding of how to guide your pet's future interactions.

Previously, I discussed leash training, which is crucial for successful public outings. Rather than avoiding areas with other people and dogs, your goal is to be able to take your dog to such places without incident.

Cavachons thrive on interaction with their humans and can be happily engaged in interesting public places like parks, walking trails, or beaches that are full of new sights, sounds, and smells. Contrary to what some people think, well-managed outings in varied environments help to create confidence in your dog.

A Cavachon will 'shut down' with any harsh correction, so having a fun and positive training session is a must - as well as very good treats (mine like liver or chicken)!

Keep training sessions short and fun and end with a game or a special toy. It is OK to be silly with a Cavachon, they enjoy it!! A high pitch to your voice and lots of love is appreciated. I say 'YES' when they do something right and give an immediate treat.

If you do use a leash, try using a separate leash for training and they will learn to tell the difference between this and a regular walking leash. Most of all, you will need patience and a sense of humor to train a Cavachon.

Dog Whispering

Many people can be confused when they need professional help with their dog because for many years, if you needed help with your dog, you contacted a 'dog trainer' or took your dog to 'puppy classes', where your dog would learn how to sit or stay.

The difference between a dog trainer and a dog whisperer would be that a dog trainer teaches a dog how to perform certain tasks, and a dog whisperer alleviates behavior problems by teaching humans what they need to do to keep their particular dog happy.

Often, depending on how soon the guardian has sought help, this can mean that the dog in question has developed some pretty serious issues, such as aggressive barking, lunging, biting, or attacking other dogs, pets, or people.

Dog whispering is often an emotional roller coaster ride for the humans involved that unveils many truths when they finally realize that it has been their actions (or inactions) that have likely caused the unbalanced behavior that their dog is now displaying. Once solutions are provided, the relief for both dog and human can be quite cathartic when they realize that with the correct direction, they can indeed live a happy life with their dog.

All specific methods of training, such as 'clicker' training, fall outside of what every dog needs to be happy, because training your dog to respond to a clicker, which you can easily do on your own, and then letting them sleep in your bed, eat from your plate, and any other multitude of things humans allow, are what makes the dog unbalanced and causes behavior problems.

I always say to people, don't wait until you have a severe problem before getting some dog whispering or professional help of some sort, because with the proper training, Man can learn to be dog's best friend.

Don't Reward Bad Behavior

It is very important to recognize that any attention paid to an out-of-control, adolescent puppy, even negative attention, is likely to be exciting and rewarding for your Cavachon puppy.

Chasing after a puppy when they have taken something they shouldn't have, picking them up when barking or showing aggression, pushing them off when they jump on other people, or yelling when they refuse to come when called are all forms of attention that can actually be rewarding for most puppies.

It will be your responsibility to provide structure for your puppy, which will include finding acceptable and safe ways to allow your puppy to vent their energy without being destructive or harmful to others.

The worst thing you can do when training your Cavachon is to yell at him or use punishment. Positive reinforcement training methods – that is, rewarding your dog for good behavior – are infinitely more effective than negative reinforcement – training by punishment.

It is important when training your Cavachon that you do not allow yourself to get frustrated. If you feel yourself starting to get angry, take a break and come back to the training session later.

Photo Credit: Linda & Steve Rogers of Timshell Farm

Why is punishment-based training so bad? Think about it this way – your dog should listen to you because he wants to please you, right?

If you train your dog using punishment, he could become fearful of you and that could put a damper on your relationship with him. Do your dog and yourself a favor by using positive reinforcement.

Teaching Basic Commands

When it comes to training your Cavachon, you have to start off slowly with the basic commands. The most popular basic commands for dogs include sit, down, stay, and come.

Sit

This is the most basic and one of the most important commands you can teach your Cavachon.

1. Stand in front of your Cavachon with a few small treats in your pocket.

2. Hold one treat in your dominant hand and wave it in front of your Cavachon's nose so he gets the scent.

3. Give the "Sit" command.

4. Move the treat upward and backward over your Cavachon's head so he is forced to raise his head to follow it.

5. In the process, his bottom will lower to the ground.

6. As soon as your Cavachon's bottom hits the ground, praise him and give him the treat.

7. Repeat this process several times until your dog gets the hang of it and responds consistently.

Down

After the "Sit" command, "Down" is the next logical command to teach because it is a progression from "Sit".

1. Kneel in front of your Cavachon with a few small treats in your pocket.

2. Hold one treat in your dominant hand and give your Cavachon the "Sit" command.

3. Reward your Cavachon for sitting, then give him the "Down" command.

4. Quickly move the treat down to the floor between your

Cavachon's paws.

5. Your dog will follow the treat and should lie down to retrieve it.

6. Praise and reward your Cavachon when he lies down.

7. Repeat this process several times until your dog gets the hang of it and responds consistently.

Come

It is very important that your Cavachon responds to a "Come" command, because there may come a time when you need to get his attention and call him to your side during a dangerous situation (such as him running around too close to traffic).

1. Put your Cavachon on a short leash and stand in front of him.

2. Give your Cavachon the "Come" command, then quickly take a few steps backward away from him.

3. Clap your hands and act excited, but do not repeat the "Come" command.

4. Keep moving backwards in small steps until your Cavachon follows and comes to you.

5. Praise and reward your Cavachon and repeat the process.

6. Over time, you can use a longer leash or take your Cavachon off the leash entirely.

7. You can also start by standing further from your Cavachon when you give the "Come" command.

8. If your Cavachon doesn't come to you immediately, you can use the leash to pull him toward you.

Stay

This command is very important because it teaches your Cavachon discipline – not only does it teach your Cavachon to stay, but it also forces him to listen and pay attention to you.

1. Find a friend to help you with this training session.

2. Have your friend hold your Cavachon on the leash while you stand in front of the dog.

3. Give your Cavachon the "Sit" command and reward him for responding correctly.

4. Give your dog the "Stay" command while holding your hand out like a "Stop" sign.

5. Take a few steps backward away from your dog and pause for 1 to 2 seconds.

6. Step back toward your Cavachon, then praise and reward your dog.

7. Repeat the process several times, then start moving back a little further before you return to your dog.

Beyond Basic Training

Once your Cavachon has a firm grasp on the basics, you can move on to teaching him additional commands. You can also add distractions to the equation to reinforce your dog's mastery of the commands. The end goal is to ensure that your Cavachon responds to your command each and every time – regardless of distractions and anything else he might rather be doing. This is incredibly important, because there may come a time when your dog is in a dangerous situation and if he doesn't respond to your command, he could get hurt.

After your Cavachon has started to respond correctly to the basic commands on a regular basis, you can start to incorporate distractions.

If you previously conducted your training sessions indoors, you might consider moving them outside where your dog could be distracted by various sights, smells, and sounds.

One thing you might try is to give your dog the Stay command and then toss a toy nearby that will tempt him to break his Stay. Start by tossing the toy at a good distance from him and wait a few seconds before you release him to play. Eventually you will be able to toss a toy right next to your dog without him breaking his Stay until you give him permission to do so.

Incorporating Hand Signals

Teaching your Cavachon to respond to hand signals in addition to verbal commands is very useful – you never know when you will be in a situation where your dog might not be able to hear you.

To start out, choose your dominant hand to give the hand signals, and hold a small treat in that hand while you are training your dog – this will encourage your dog to focus on your hand during training, and it will help to cement the connection between the command and the hand signal.

To begin, give your dog the Sit or Down command while holding the treat in your dominant hand and give the appropriate hand signal – for Sit you might try a closed fist and for Down, you might place your hand flat, parallel to the ground.

When your dog responds correctly, give him the treat. You will need to repeat this process many times in order for your dog to form a connection between both the verbal command and the hand signal with the desired behavior.

Eventually, you can start to remove the verbal command from the equation – use the hand gesture every time, but start to use the verbal command only half the time.

Once your dog gets the hang of this, you should start to remove the food reward from the equation. Continue to give your dog the hand signal for each command, and occasionally use the verbal command just to remind him.

You should start to phase out the food rewards, however, by offering them only half the time. Progressively lessen the use of the food reward, but continue to praise your dog for performing the behavior correctly so he learns to repeat it.

Teaching Distance Commands

In addition to getting your dog to respond to hand signals, it is also useful to teach him to respond to your commands even when you are not directly next to him.

This may come in handy if your dog is running around outside and gets too close to the street – you should be able to give him a Sit or Down command so he stops before he gets into a dangerous situation.

Photo Credit: Lynn Millar.

Teaching your dog distance commands is not difficult, but it does require some time and patience.

To start, give your Cavachon a brief refresher course of the basic commands while you are standing or kneeling right next to him.

Next, give your dog the Sit and Stay commands, then move a few feet away before you give the Come command.

Repeat this process, increasing the distance between you and your dog before giving him the Come command. Be sure to praise and reward your dog for responding appropriately when he does so.

Once your dog gets the hang of coming on command from a distance, you can start to incorporate other commands. One method of doing so is to teach your dog to sit when you grab his collar. To do so, let your dog wander freely and every once in a while walk up and grab his collar while giving the Sit command.

After a few repetitions, your dog should begin to respond with a Sit when you grab his collar, even if you do not give the command.

Gradually, you can increase the distance from which you come to grab his collar and give him the command.

After your dog starts to respond consistently when you come from a distance to grab his collar, you can start giving the Sit command without moving toward him.

It may take your dog a few times to get the hang of it, so be patient. If your dog doesn't sit right away, calmly walk up to him and repeat the Sit command, but do not grab his collar this time.

Eventually, your dog will get the hang of it, and you can start to practice using other commands like Down and Stay from a distance.

Clicker Training

To help speed up the training process for your Cavachon you might want to look into clicker training. Clicker training is a version of positive reinforcement training.

When it comes to training your Cavachon, you are going to be most successful if you maintain consistency. Unless you are very clear with your dog about what your expectations are, he may simply decide not to follow your commands.

A simple way to achieve consistency in training your Cavachon is to use the principles of clicker training. Clicker training involves using a small handheld device that makes a clicking noise when you press it between your fingers.

Clicker training is based on the theory of operant conditioning, which helps your dog to make the connection between the desired behavior and the offering of a reward.

Cavachons have a natural desire to please, so if they learn that a certain behavior earns your approval, they will be eager to repeat it – clicker training is a great way to help your dog quickly identify the particular behavior you want him to repeat.

All you have to do is give your Cavachon a command and, as soon as he performs the behavior, you use the clicker. After you use the clicker, give your dog the reward as you would with any form of positive reinforcement training.

You should only use the clicker for the first few times to make sure that your Cavachon doesn't become dependent on the sound to perform the behavior.

Make sure you praise your dog every time he performs the desired behavior. Cavachons are people pleasers, so if they learn that something they do makes you happy, they will be eager to repeat it.

Use food rewards during the early stages of training for positive reinforcement, but phase them out after your Cavachon gets the hang of each command.

Some of the benefits of clicker training include:

• Very easy to implement – all you need is the clicker.

• Helps your dog form a connection between the command and the desired behavior more quickly.

• You only need to use the clicker until your dog makes the connection, then you can stop.

• May help to keep your dog's attention more effectively if he hears the noise.

Clicker training is just one method of positive reinforcement training that you can consider for training your Cavachon. No matter what method you choose, it is important that you maintain consistency and always praise and reward your dog for responding to your commands correctly so he learns to repeat the behavior.

First Tricks

When teaching your Cavachon their first tricks, in order to give them extra incentive, find a small treat that they would do anything to get, and give the treat as a reward to help solidify a good performance.

Most dogs will be extra attentive during training sessions when they know that they will be rewarded with their favorite treats.

Photo Credit: Barby Wolfish of Pet Pointe.

If your Cavachon is less than six months old when you begin teaching them tricks, keep your training sessions short (no more than 5 or 10 minutes) and make the sessions lots of fun.

As your Cavachon becomes an adult, you can extend your sessions because they will be able to maintain their focus for longer periods of time.

Playing Dead

Once your Cavachon knows the command to 'lie down', which should be one of the basic obedience commands he learns at 'school', getting him to 'play dead' is simple.

Once the dog is lying down, hold a treat in front of your pet close enough for him to smell it. Move the treat in circles toward the floor giving your Cavachon the command, 'Play Dead'.

The motion should encourage the dog to roll over on his back. As soon as he achieves the correct position, praise him and give him the treat. Cavachons love treats so much, it won't take your pet long to put it all together and execute the maneuver on command.

Shake a Paw

Who doesn't love a dog who knows how to shake a paw? This is one of the easiest tricks to teach your Cavachon.

Practice every day until they are 100% reliable with this trick, and then it will be time to add another trick to their repertoire.

Most dogs are naturally either right or left pawed. If you know which paw your dog favors, ask them to shake this paw.

Find a quiet place to practice, without noisy distractions or other pets, and stand or sit in front of your dog. Place them in the sitting position and hold a treat in your left hand.

Say the command 'Shake' while putting your right hand behind their left or right paw and pulling the paw gently toward yourself until you are holding their paw in your hand. Immediately praise them and give them the treat.

Most dogs will learn the 'Shake' trick very quickly, and in no time at all, once you put out your hand, your Cavachon will immediately lift their paw and put it into your hand without your assistance or any verbal cue.

Give Me Five

The next trick after 'Shake' should be 'High Five'. Teach this sequence the same way, but when you hold out your hand to shake, move your hand up and touch your dog's paw saying, 'High five!'. It may take a few tries, but by this time your Cavachon will be getting the idea that if he learns his lessons, he gets his treat.

This set of four tricks is a good example of using one behavior to build to another. Almost any dog can be taught to perform basic tricks, but don't lose sight of the fact that you are dealing with an individual personality. You may have a Cavachon that would rather chase his chew toys than learn 'routines'. Get to know what your dog enjoys doing and follow his lead to build his unique set of tricks.

Roll Over

You will find that just like your Cavachon is naturally either right or left pawed, that they will also naturally want to roll to either the right or the left side.

Take advantage of this by asking your dog to roll to the side they naturally prefer. Sit with your dog on the floor and put them in a lying down position.

Hold a treat in your hand and place it close to their nose without allowing them to grab it, and while they are in the lying position, move the treat to the right or left side of their head so that they have to roll over to get to it.

You will quickly see which side they want to naturally roll to; once you see this, move the treat to that side. Once they roll over to that side, immediately give them the treat and praise them.

You can say the verbal cue 'Over' while you demonstrate the hand signal motion (moving your right hand in a half circular motion) from one side of their head to the other.

Sit Pretty

While this trick is a little more complicated, and most dogs pick up on it very quickly, remember that this trick requires balance, and every dog is different, so always exercise patience.

Find a quiet space with few distractions and sit or stand in front of your dog and ask them to 'Sit'.

Have a treat nearby (on a countertop or table) and when they sit, use both of your hands to lift up their front paws into the sitting pretty position, while saying the command 'Sit Pretty'. Help them balance in this position while you praise them and give them the treat.

Once your Cavachon can do the balancing part of the trick quite easily without your help, sit or stand in front of your dog while asking them to 'Sit Pretty' and hold the treat above their head, at the level their nose would be when they sit pretty.

If they attempt to stand on their back legs to get the treat, you may be holding the treat too high, which will encourage them to stand up on their back legs to reach it. Go back to the first step and put them back into the 'Sit' position, and again lift their paws while their backside remains on the floor.

The hand signal for 'Sit Pretty' is a straight arm held over your dog's head with a closed fist. Place your Cavachon beside a wall when first teaching this trick so that they can use the wall to help their balance.

A young Cavachon puppy should be able to easily learn these basic tricks before they are six months old, and when you are patient and make your training sessions short and fun for your dog, they will be eager to learn more.

Excessive Jumping

Allowing any dog to jump up on a person is a serious mistake and can be a health risk for Cavachons, placing too much pressure and twisting force on their spines. Beyond this fact, dogs that jump are simply obnoxious. They knock things and people over with their exuberance and cause damaging by scratching.

Fortunately the Cavachon jumps no more than other breeds. Jumping is one of the most undesirable of all traits in a dog, especially if the animal has muddy paws or is meeting a frail person. Many people are afraid of dogs, and find spontaneous jumping threatening.

Don't make the mistake of assuming that excessive jumping is an expression of friendliness. All too often it's a case of a dominant dog asserting his authority and saying, "I don't respect you".

Dogs that know their proper place in the 'pack' don't jump on more dominant dogs. A jumper sees himself as the 'top dog' in all situations.

As the dog's master, you must enforce the 'no jumping' rule. Anything else will only confuse your pet. Dogs have a keen perception of space. Rather than retreating from a jumping dog, step sideways and forward, taking back your space that he is trying to claim.

You are not trying to knock your dog down, but he may careen into

you and fall anyway. Again, always keep in mind the potential for damage to the Cavachon's spinal cord and exercise appropriate judgment. Remain casual and calm. Take slow, deliberate motions and protect the 'bubble' around your body. Your dog won't be expecting this action from you, and won't enjoy it.

Photo Credit: Linda & Steve Rogers of Timshell Farm.

After several failed jumps, the dog will lose interest when his dominant message is no longer getting across.

It is important to praise him when he does have all four feet on the ground. Rewarding good behavior is often forgotten.

Linda Kaiser of Smooch My Pups adds: "How do you deal with a Cavachon that excessively jumps up at people? Let's begin by saying that you have to establish right away who the pack leader is.

This is KEY in all aspects of owning an obedient, respectful dog. Please keep in mind that dogs understand dog language. If a momma dog has an issue with her young, she would never tolerate it. If she sees something she doesn't like, she will move the puppy in a calm assertive manner, out of the way. She uses her body to teach boundaries. You can use yours too. When you have a dog that habitually jumps up, he/she is establishing that they are your pack leader. Gain control of this by teaching your dog simple commands. This is imperative to having a great, social member of society. When you come in and you are greeted by your dog, make him sit before being petted. If he jumps on you, softly meet him/her with a raised knee, a firm 'OFF' and follow with the command 'SIT'. Praise your dog when you get the desired results. You must be consistent!! Remember, you also must establish from the beginning (puppy stage) that you are the pack leader. A pack leader never negotiates. If you are inconsistent it could lead to role reversal, creating a dog that is confused, nervous, anxious and one that may never be house trainable. Think like a dog and you will be very successful at being TOP DOG!"

Barking Behavior

Of course your Cavachon will bark, but there is a point where it can become excessive, creating serious problems, especially if you live near other people. If you are in an apartment complex with shared walls, a barking dog can get you thrown out of your home. To get to the bottom of problem barking, you must first try to figure out what is setting your dog off. Your Cavachon may bark for the following reasons:

Boredom — Being left alone for long periods causes sadness.

Fear — They may sense a threat such as another animal.

Greeting — They love to greet visitors, or perhaps on a walk they want to communicate with another dog. This would usually be accompanied with a wagging tail and maybe jumping up.

Getting Attention — He may need to go outside to go to the toilet, or maybe he wants attention from you or food.

So what can you do when you have an issue?

1. Nip it in the bud by dealing with barking problems as quickly as possible before it escalates.

2. Fence your garden or yard with solid fencing so he feels safer and less threatened.

3. Ignore your Cavachon until he stops barking. You don't want him thinking he can just bark and get what he wants, or he will only keep repeating the behavior.

4. If he barks while you're out and the neighbors complain, he is bored. Don't leave him as long; get someone to come in and play with him or leave toys that occupy him.

5. As with all problem behaviors, address barking with patience and consistency. Don't shout and get angry — he will bark even louder.

6. You can feed him a treat AFTER as a reward but never when he is barking, otherwise he will start to bark to get a treat!

7. For real problem barkers, humane bark collars can teach the dog through negative reinforcement. These collars release a harmless spray of citronella into the dog's nose in response to vibrations in the throat. The system, though somewhat expensive at $100/£60, works in almost all cases.

Linda Kaiser of Smooch My Pups adds: "This is a natural way of communication for our pets. It is important that you are always the pack leader. Every habit picked up by dogs can be easily corrected if you maintain this status early on. It is the language that dogs can understand and relate to. A lot of times, excess barking is a result of pent up or excess energy. Take lots of time to interact with your dog and the problems that arise from a frustrated dog will be fewer. When a dog is barking, divert their attention. Hopefully you have been consistent in your interaction with your dog and you have established some simple commands. If you haven't, this is a good place to start. Teach sit, down, stay, off, and come/recall. Once you have these commands successfully instilled in your dog, the command 'QUIET' will be a lot easier. The use of a leash if your dog is outside or inside is very helpful. You can grab the leash and divert his/her attention while they are barking by grabbing the leash and redirecting their attention to you with a command of 'NO BARK' or 'Quiet', whichever you prefer. I can't stress enough how consistency is key, along with having already established your alpha status. If you are unsuccessful at teaching these commands please seek the advice of a professional."

Chewing

Chewing is a natural behavior in dogs and one that Cavachons take to the extreme. If left undirected, the dogs are capable of causing unbelievable levels of destruction in your home.

Normal chewing relieves anxiety, keeps their jaws strong and their teeth clean. However, excessive chewing indicates some combination of anxiety or boredom, which may mean you need to get your dog out of the house more. Make sure you are giving your Cavachon plenty of physical and mental stimulation by taking him to the dog park, playing games such as fetch, or enrolling him in activities such as agility training.

Puppies go through a teething stage like human babies where they lose their baby teeth and experience pain as their adult teeth grow through. This should be done with by about six months, but before then you can still channel your puppy's urge to chew in the right direction. Make sure your dog has proper chew toys that exist to be destroyed! Keep things interesting by buying new ones every so often.

Yes, you can give him a bone, but only natural bones that are sold specifically for chewing, because cooked bones can splinter and seriously injure him.

If you catch your pet chewing on a forbidden object, reprimand (we don't mean punish) him and take the item away. Immediately substitute an appropriate chew toy and if you chose to, reward him with attention or a treat.

You can buy chewing deterrents such as Grannick's Bitter Apple spray which you spray on all objects that you don't want your dog to chew. Reapply the deterrent every day for two to four weeks.

Linda Kaiser of Smooch My Pups adds: "We have to be mindful of the fact that from 3-8 weeks puppies are getting their deciduous teeth. Those teeth will then be replaced by their permanent teeth from 4-6 months. These are the times that chewing is at its most painful. Their gums are very irritated, and chewing is their natural instinct at this time. This can lead to a long standing problem, however, if you do not get it under control. Please always rule out any potential medical problem causing the excess chewing. Always maintain alpha dog status. This will help with them chewing your belongings. Puppy proof your home. Do not let puppy have free access to your home, and never unsupervised. Provide acceptable chew items, like raw bones, antlers, and perhaps a Kong with organic peanut butter in it. Never feed cooked bones or rawhide and always supervise your dog when he has something to chew on. Deter your dog from chewing on unacceptable items with replacement of acceptable things. Dogs benefit greatly from exercise. A dog that is stimulated with exercise is usually one that will rest when play time or walk time is over."

Digging

Digging indoors, like barking and chewing, can be an expression of fear, anxiety, and/or boredom. Digging is a difficult behavior to stop. The best solution is to spend more time playing with and exercising your pet and providing your dog with an outdoor sandbox where digging is allowed. Also, consider enrolling your pet in a dog daycare facility so he will not be alone while you are at work and thus will be less susceptible to separation anxiety.

Begging

Any dog will beg at the table if allowed to do so. My best advice to you is to never allow this behavior to get started. Make 'people food' off limits from day one. If your pet becomes a serious beggar, confine him to another part of the house during meal times. This is as a control measure for you and other people at the table. If you can't ignore a plaintive, begging set of Cavachon eyes, you're the real problem!

Biting

Cavachons can be problem biters, especially when they are stressed or being aggressive over their territory – including you. Try to curb nipping and biting from puppyhood forward and make sure your dog is exposed to a wide range of environments and circumstances.

Photo Credit: Linda & Steve Rogers of Timshell Farm.

With their littermates, your Cavachon would have learned about bite inhibition, which is a dog's ability to control the pressure he uses when biting so that he doesn't cause pain or harm. When puppies are playing, if they bite too hard the other puppy will yelp or run away, which teaches the puppy not to bite so hard. This would have curbed the rough play, and this technique can be used when this nipping becomes painful or dangerous to you.

If your Cavachon puppy has a tendency to bite you a little harder than you think he should, you can teach him bite inhibition yourself. When playing with your puppy if he bites you, you should say "Ouch!" in a calm tone and gently remove your hand from his mouth to imitate the reaction as if from a sibling in the pack. After you do, stop paying attention to the puppy for a few seconds before resuming play. It may also be helpful for you to give your puppy a chew toy after removing your hand so he learns what he is and is not allowed to chew on.

Obviously, any dog will bite if he is reacting out of pain or fear. Biting is a dog's primary means of defense. Use socialization, obedience training, and stern corrections to control a puppy's playful nips. If an adult dog displays biting behavior, it is imperative to get to the bottom of the biting. Have the dog evaluated for a health problem and work with a professional trainer.

Dealing with Copraphagia

Copraphagia is when dogs eat feces, either their own or that of another animal. While we may be appalled at this, it is actually quite common in dogs. The problem is that nobody really seems to know why this happens. Reasons speculated upon include a lack of nutrition in their diet, being left alone, or learned behavior from their time in the litter. Mostly they will grow out of this, but how can we discourage it?

1. Clean up after him as soon as he has eliminated.

2. Keep him stimulated with chew toys and games and don't leave him alone for long periods.

3. Review his diet — Vitamin-B deficiency is a key suspect, but it could be another nutrient he is lacking.

4. You could feed certain foods that are expelled and smell disgusting to him so he avoids eating them. These include parsley, and courgettes/zucchinis.

Chapter 10 – Keeping Your Cavachon Healthy

This chapter is intended to give owners an indication of some of the common illnesses that may affect their Cavachon. For legal reasons, I have to put in the disclaimer that I am not a qualified veterinarian, and if you have any concerns regarding the health of your dog, you should immediately consult a veterinarian.

You are your Cavachon's primary healthcare provider. You will know what is 'normal' for your dog. Yours will be the best sense that something is wrong, even when there is no obvious injury or illness. The more you understand preventive health care, the better you will care for your dog throughout his life.

First Visit to the Vet

Working with a qualified veterinarian is critical to long-term and comprehensive healthcare. If you do not already have a vet, ask

your breeder for a recommendation. If you purchased your pet outside your area, contact your local dog club and ask for referrals.

Make an appointment to tour the clinic and meet the vet. Be clear about the purpose of your visit and about your intent to pay the regular office fee. Don't expect to get a freebie interview, and don't waste anyone's time! Go in with a set of prepared questions. Be sure to cover the following points:

- How long has this practice been in operation?
- How many vets are on staff?
- Are any of your doctors specialists?
- If not, to which doctors do you refer patients?
- What are your regular business hours?
- Do you recommend a specific emergency clinic?
- Do you have emergency hours?
- What specific medical services do you offer?
- Do you offer grooming services?
- May I have an estimated schedule of fees?

- Do you currently treat any Cavachons?

Pay attention to all aspects of your visit, including how the facilities appear, and the demeanor of the staff. Things to look for include:

- How the staff interacts with clients
- The degree of organization or lack thereof
- Indications of engagement with the clientele (office bulletin board, cards and photos displayed, etc.)
- Quality of all visible equipment
- Cleanliness of the waiting area and back rooms
- Prominent display of doctors' credentials

These are only some suggestions. Go with your gut. If the clinic and staff seems to 'feel' right to you, trust your instincts. If not, no matter how well appointed the practice may appear to be, visit more clinics before making a decision.

When you are comfortable with a vet practice, schedule a second visit to include your Cavachon puppy. Bring all the dog's medical records. Be ready to discuss completing vaccinations and having the animal spayed or neutered.

Routine exam procedures include temperature and a check of heart and lung function with a stethoscope. The vet will weigh and measure the puppy. These baseline numbers will help chart growth and physical progress. If you have specific questions, prepare them in advance.

Spaying and Neutering

Most reputable Cavachon sales are conducted by way of spay/neuter contracts which stipulate that spaying or neutering is to be completed after the puppy has reached sexual maturity.

Females can get pregnant in old age — they don't go through a menopause. Spaying is the removal of her ovaries and womb (uterus).

Neutering is the removal of the male's testicles, also known as castration, in what is a routine operation. Yes, of course he will feel tender and slightly sore, but this will last only a few days.

Ask yourself, why wouldn't you have these procedures done unless of course you are planning to breed? Don't be swayed by popular misconceptions (myths) such as the operation will subdue or permanently affect his character and personality, or that the dog

will gain weight. Remember that dogs are not humans; their need for sex is purely physical, caused by hormones that when removed will mean your dog does not desire or miss sex.

Photo Credit: Celia M Evans of Scarletstrue.

It is very important that spay/neuter procedures are done **after sexual maturity** because there is ongoing emotional maturing that needs to take place. This maturation happens during the final phase of puppy adolescence (usually 9 months to 12 months old) and helps to achieve healthy, balanced adult Cavachon behavior. Sexual maturity happens after a first menstrual cycle, often referred to as being 'in heat' or 'in season', and takes place in the bitch puppy and after the male dog is capable of having the ability to sire pups.

A female Cavachon will have her menstrual cycle every 6/8 months on average, and this lasts usually 12-21 days. Her hormones will be raging, and through a sense of smell hundreds of times more powerful than ours, the male dogs from miles around will be on alert. You will notice some bleeding (spotting). This is perfectly normal.

Spay and neuter procedures may also carry some health and behavioral benefits:

1. Neutering reduces the risk of prostatic disease or perianal tumors in male dogs.

2. The surgery may also lessen aggressive behaviors, territorial urine marking, and inappropriate mounting.

3. Spayed females have a diminished risk for breast cancer and no prospect of uterine or ovarian cancer.

4. There is no possibility of an unplanned or unwanted litter.

5. There are no mood swings related to hormones or issues (such as mess) around the bitch coming into season.

6. No unintentional litters from females being bred.

Nichola Lack of Cracking Cavachons: "Costs on spay/neuter here in the UK vary greatly from vet to vet. On average you are looking at £160. I would not spay/neuter under 12 months of age and would much prefer 18 months to 2 years. A dog should be fully mature, mentally and physically."

Linda Kaiser of Smooch My Pups: "Costs in the USA for spaying and neutering are all over the board....some as little as $80 all the way up to as much as $300 in most states. While there is scientific fact to support that early spaying/neutering can drastically reduce certain cancers, it isn't always clear if reports are done in perspective to lactating females or just the female population in general. Most reports that I have came across don't clarify that. It has been stated that female dogs that are spayed prior to their first heat cycle will reduce her risk of getting mammary cancer to zero percent. In the human world, a nursing mom has less of a risk in getting breast cancer if she nurses her baby. That is why I question whether or not the scientists are lumping all females into the percentages and reporting on that statistic, using a play on words. Very controversial indeed! That being said, of course if you remove reproductive organs you are not going to get cancer in them. Hence the other statistic, that the risk of uterine cancer is less if spayed earlier. This same logic I also believe for the male dog. If you remove their testicles they will have zero percent chance of getting testicular cancer!! Ok, so there may be some benefit to behavioral problems by early removal of hormones, but I firmly believe those also can be eradicated if you are a strong alpha role model. This doesn't mean you have to be mean or aggressive to your dog. This means being a clear, decisive leader. In my opinion, the next cause for concern of early spaying or neutering is the lack of development, of the overall health of our dogs, resulting from taking away essential hormones. It has recently been discovered that doing so can lead to joint and ligament issues. I personally have heard of more dogs having problems with patellas, hips, torn ACLs, etc. My concern is that this is related to not allowing the dog's natural growth to take place before you take away important hormones they need to grow properly. I know that growth platelets don't even close until between 4-8 months, so why would you risk desexing before that time frame? It's just another door that is opened for a problem to arise. This principle is also true concerning other joints and ligaments. I firmly believe and teach my clients to wait until their puppy has fully matured to do any physical altering. Sometimes that means they wait until they are over 1 year of age."

Vaccinations

If your Cavachon puppy is not immunized, then he is at risk from potentially fatal canine diseases because he has no protection. Contact with other dogs could occur at parks or at the vets, so be very careful until he has received his first vaccinations. After birth, puppies receive immunity to many diseases from their mother's milk (this is called colostrums), but as they mature, this immunity fades.

Without immunization, your pup won't be covered under any pet insurance policy you may have taken out.

To give a balanced view, I will also point out that some breeders believe some Cavachons are **'over-vaccinated'** and while very rare, there is the possibility of a reaction to the vaccine too.

A minor reaction could affect your Cavachon in ways such as making them sleepy, sneeze, irritable, and especially sore or developing a lump where injected. These should resolve in a few days.

A more severe reaction requiring immediate treatment would include vomiting, diarrhea, seizures, and a hypersensitivity reaction similar to that of a human anaphylactic reaction.

So what are the worst threats? There are two deadly threats that are the main focus of the initial vaccinations — distemper and parvo virus.

Distemper causes flu-like symptoms initially and progresses to severe painful neurological symptoms such as seizures and often ends in death. The virus is airborne so can be caught if your puppy comes into close proximity of an infected dog.

Parvo virus causes diarrhea and vomiting, often ending in death. The virus can be present in grass or on other surfaces for years.

A puppy's recommended vaccinations begin at 6-7 weeks of age. The most common combination vaccine given is known as **DHPP**. The initials refer to the diseases included in the vaccine — Distemper, Hepatitis, Parvo, and Parainfluenza. Some vets may also include protection against Coronavirus and the bacteria Leptospirosis at the same time. The first injection thereby protects him from a number of diseases in one go.

In the UK, this first vaccinations tends to include: Distemper, Canine Parvovirus (Parvo), Infectious Canine Hepatitis (Adenovirus), Leptospirosis, and Kennel Cough (Bordetella).

Why the differences? Canine Coronavirus is a relatively new vaccine and so is not offered as standard in every veterinary practice in the UK. Rabies is considered to have been eliminated within the UK, however, if you plan to take your dog out of the country, you will require a pet passport and then they must be vaccinated against rabies.

Recommended boosters occur at 9, 12, and 16 weeks. In some geographical regions in the USA, a vaccine for Lyme disease (typically in forested areas) starts at 16 weeks with a booster at 18 weeks.

The rabies vaccination is administered at 12-16 weeks and yearly for life thereafter, although many states allow 3 years between rabies vaccinations.

Most vaccinations are administered by means of an injection, although kennel cough is usually administered using a nasal spray.

Once this initial schedule has been completed, the debate opens up over the frequency of boosters. General practice is to give a distemper/parvo booster a year after the completion of their puppy series. After that, it depends on the individual vet, but usually a booster takes place every three years after the completion of the initial puppy series.

Once your puppy has had their second set of vaccines, they should be safe to go into the outside world and play with other dogs.

Some of our breeders are in favor of a titer test. This is a straightforward blood test that measures a dog's antibodies to vaccine viruses. Titers accurately assess protection against the core diseases in dogs, enabling veterinarians to judge whether a booster vaccination is really necessary.

TIP - On vaccinations, I would suggest people need to speak with their vets about local requirements, but be mindful of the latest WSAVA advice, which has moved away from 'annual boosters' for everything. WSAVA stands for The World Small Animal Veterinary Association. Its membership is made up of global veterinary organizations: http://www.wsava.org/

Victoria Johnson of Cosmic Cavachons & Cavapoos says: "Nosodes are a homeopathic alternative to vaccines and can be purchased from most homeopathic online stores, including Ainsworth and Helios or a homeopathic vet."

Evaluating for Worms

Puppies purchased from a breeder are almost always parasite-free because puppies are given their first dose of worming medication at around two weeks old, then again at five and eight weeks before they leave the litter. This is another reason to make sure you buy from a reputable breeder and not someone who doesn't know what they are doing. Worms are more common in rescue dogs, strays, and from 'backyard breeders'.

I have talked about taking your Cavachon to the vet within days of your purchase to get him health checked. A worm test is usually done then. These tests are important because some parasites, like tapeworms, may be life threatening. Your vet will need a fecal sample for this purpose.

The main types of worms affecting puppies are **roundworm** and **tapeworm**. Roundworms appear as small white granules around the anus. Other types of worms can only be seen through a microscope.

If the puppy tests positive, the standard treatment is a deworming agent with a follow-up dose in 10 days. Most vets recommend worming a puppy once a month until he is six months old, and then around every two or three months.

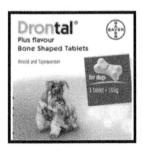

Dangers to you: Roundworm can pass from a puppy to humans, in the most severe cases causing blindness or miscarriage in women. Make sure you wash your hands immediately after handling your puppy.

Heartworms

Mosquitoes spread heartworms (*Dirofilaria Immitis*) through their bites. They are thin, long parasites that infest the muscles of the heart, where they block blood vessels and cause bleeding. Their presence can lead to heart failure and death. Coughing and fainting, as well as an intolerance to exercise, are all symptoms of heartworm. Discuss heartworm prevention with your vet and decide on the best course of action to keep your pet safe.

Warning Signs of Illness in Your Cavachon

- excessive and unexplained drooling
- excessive consumption of water and increased urination
- changes in appetite leading to weight gain or loss
- marked change in levels of activity
- disinterest in favorite activities
- stiffness and difficulty standing or climbing stairs
- sleeping more than normal
- shaking of the head
- any sores, lumps, or growths
- dry, red, or cloudy eyes

Often the signs of serious illness are subtle. Trust your instincts. If you think something is wrong, do not hesitate to consult with your vet.

'Normal' Health Issues

Although Cavachons are vigorous, healthy dogs, all canines can face medical issues. The following are 'normal' health-related matters that may need veterinary evaluation. Pets that are inattentive or lethargic and that are not eating or drinking should be examined. None of these behaviors are normal for a Cavachon.

Diarrhea

Cavachon puppies, like all small dogs, are subject to digestive upsets. Puppies just will get into things they shouldn't, like human food or even the kitchen garbage. Diarrhea from these causes resolves within 24 hours.

During that time, the puppy should have only small portions of dry food and no treats. Give the dog lots of fresh, clean water to guard against dehydration. If the loose, watery stools are still present after 24 hours, take your Cavachon to the vet.

The same period of watchful waiting applies for adult dogs. If episodic diarrhea becomes chronic, take a good look at your pet's diet. Chances are good that the dog is getting too much rich, fatty food and needs less fat and protein. Some dogs also do better eating small amounts of food several times a day rather than having 2-3 larger meals.

Allergy testing can identify the causes of some cases of diarrhea. Many small dogs are allergic to chicken and turkey. A change in diet resolves their gastrointestinal upset immediately. Diets based on rabbit or duck are often used for dogs with such intolerances.

Either a bacteria or a virus can cause diarrhea, which accompanies fever and vomiting. Parasites, in particular tapeworms and roundworms, may also be to blame.

Vomiting

Dietary changes or the puppy 'getting into something' can also cause vomiting. Again, this should resolve within 24 hours. If the dog tries to vomit but can't bring anything up, vomits blood, or can't keep water down, take your pet to the vet immediately.

Dehydration from vomiting occurs faster than in a case of diarrhea, and can be fatal. It is possible that your dog may need intravenous fluids.

When your dog is vomiting, always have a good look around to identify what, if anything, the dog may have chewed and swallowed. This can be a huge benefit in targeting appropriate treatment.

Other potential culprits include: hookworm, roundworm, pancreatitis, diabetes, thyroid disease, kidney disease, liver disease, or a physical blockage.

Bloat

Any dog can suffer from bloat. The condition is the second most common cause of death in dogs, behind cancer.

Some breeds are at higher risk than others. Also known as gastric dilation / volvulus or GDV, bloat cannot be treated with an antibiotic or prevented with a vaccine. In roughly 50% of cases, bloat is fatal.

In severe cases, the stomach twists partially or completely. This causes circulation problems throughout the digestive system. Dogs that do not receive treatment go into cardiac arrest. Even if surgical intervention is attempted, there is no guarantee of success.

Signs of bloat are often mistaken for indications of excess gas. The dog may salivate and attempt to vomit, pace, and whine. Gas reduction products at this stage can be helpful. As the stomach swells, it places pressure on surrounding vital organs, and may

burst. All cases of bloat are a *serious* **medical emergency.**

Photo Credit: Liz Priebe owner of Brody and Oliver.

Larger dogs with deep chests and small waists face a greater risk of developing bloat. These include the Great Dane, Weimaraner, Saint Bernard, Irish Setter, and the Standard Poodle. Despite being a smaller-sized dog, the Cavachon is unfortunately also at risk.

Eating habits also factor into the equation. Dogs that eat one large meal per day consisting of dry food are in a high-risk category. Feed three small meals throughout the day instead. This helps to prevent gulping, which leads to ingesting large amounts of air.

If your Cavachon is on a dry food diet, **don't** let him drink lots of water after eating. Doing so causes the dry food in the stomach to expand, leading to discomfort, and a dilution of the digestive juices. Limit the amount of play and exercise after meals. A slow walk promotes digestion, but a vigorous romp can be dangerous.

Stress also contributes to bloat, especially in anxious or nervous dogs. Changes in routine, confrontations with other dogs, and moving to a new home can all trigger an attack.

Dogs between the ages of four and seven are at an increased risk. Bloat occurs most often between 2 a.m. and 6 a.m., roughly 10 hours after the animal has had his dinner.

Test your dog's dry food by putting a serving in a bowl with water. Leave the material to expand overnight. If the degree of added bulk seems excessive, consider switching to a premium or organic food.

Keep an anti-gas medicine with simethicone on hand (consult with your veterinarian on correct dosage). Consider adding a **probiotic** to your dog's food to reduce gas in the stomach and to improve digestive health.

If a dog experiences bloat once, his risk of a future episode is greater. Keep copies of his medical records at home, and know the location of the nearest emergency vet clinic.

Allergies

Like humans, dogs also suffer from allergies, and Cavachons seem especially prone to such problems with roughly 1 in 10 being affected at some stage of their life. Food, airborne particles, and materials that touch the skin can all cause negative reactions as well as reactions to flea bites.

Owners tend to notice changes in behavior that suggest discomfort like itching. Common symptoms include chewing or biting of the tail, stomach, or hind legs, or licking of the paws.

In reaction to inhaled substances, the dog will sneeze, cough, or experience watering eyes. Ingested substances may lead to vomiting or diarrhea. Dogs can also suffer from rashes or a case of hives. Your poor Cavachon can be just as miserable as you are during an allergy attack.

If the reaction occurs in the spring or fall, the likely culprit is seasonal pollen or, in the case of hot weather, fleas. Food additives like beef, corn, wheat, soybeans, and dairy products can all cause gastrointestinal upset.

As with any allergy, remove suspect items or try a special diet. Allergy testing offers a definitive diagnosis and pinpoints necessary environmental and dietary changes. The tests are expensive, costing $200+ / £120+.

The vet may recommend medication, or bathing the dog in cool, soothing water. Special diets are also extremely helpful.

For acne-like chin rashes, switch to stainless steel, glass, or ceramic food dishes. Plastic feeding dishes cause this rash, which looks like blackheads surrounded by inflamed skin. Wash the dog's face in clear, cool water and ask the vet for an antibiotic cream to speed the healing process.

Coughing and/or Wheezing

Occasional coughing is not a cause for concern, but if it goes on for more than a week, a vet visit is in order. A cough may indicate:

- kennel cough
- heartworm
- cardiac disease
- bacterial infections
- parasites
- tumors
- allergies

The upper respiratory condition called '**kennel cough**' presents with dry hacking. It is a form of canine bronchitis caused by warm, overcrowded conditions with poor ventilation. In most cases, kennel cough resolves on its own.

Consult with your veterinarian. The doctor may prescribe a cough suppressant or suggest the use of a humidifier to soothe your pet's irritated airways.

When the cause of a cough is unclear, the vet will take a full medical history and order tests, including blood work and X-rays. Fluid may also be drawn from the lungs for analysis. Among other conditions, the doctor will be attempting to rule out heartworms.

If your dog has a heart murmur, they may cough. Get a chest X-ray to see if the heart is enlarged.

Dental Care

Chewing is a dog's only means of maintaining his teeth. Many of our canine friends develop dental problems early in life because they don't get enough of this activity. Not all dogs are prone to cavities.

Most do suffer from accumulations of plaque and associated gum diseases. Often, severe halitosis (bad breath) is the first sign that something is wrong.

Photo Credit - KoKo from Melanie McCarthy of Cavachons From The Monarchy.

With dental problems, gingivitis develops first and, if unaddressed, progresses to periodontitis. Warning signs of gum disease include:

- a reluctance to finish meals
- extreme bad breath
- swollen and bleeding gums

- irregular gum line
- plaque build-up
- drooling, and/or loose teeth

Cavachons are prone to developing gum and tooth disease because their jaws tend to be small and often their teeth are crowded. The bacterial gum infection periodontitis causes inflammation, gum recession, and possible tooth loss. It requires treatment with antibiotics to prevent a spread of the infection to other parts of the body. Symptoms include:

- pus at the gum line
- loss of appetite
- depression
- irritability
- pawing at the mouth
- trouble chewing
- loose or missing teeth
- gastrointestinal upset

Treatment begins with a professional cleaning. This procedure may also involve root work, descaling, and even extractions.

With Proliferating Gum Disease, the gums overgrow the teeth, causing inflammation and infection. Other symptoms include:

- thickening and lengthening of the gums
- bleeding
- bad breath
- drooling
- loss of appetite

The vet will prescribe antibiotics, and surgery is usually required.

Home Dental Care

There are many products available to help with home dental care for your Cavachon. Some owners opt for water additives that break up tartar and plaque, but in some cases dogs experience stomach upset. Dental sprays and wipes are also an option, but so is gentle gum massage to help break up plaque and tartar.

Most owners incorporate some type of dental chew in their standard care practices. Greenies Dental Chews for Dogs are  popular and well tolerated in a digestive sense. An added plus is that dogs usually love them. The treats come in different sizes and are priced in a range of $7 / £4.21 for 22 "Teeny Greenies" and $25 / £15 for 17 "Large Greenies".

Indigenous Dental Health Bones are safe and highly digestible for all dog breeds and sizes. They are made with ascophyllum nodosum, a natural kelp harvested from the clean, cold North Atlantic seas of Canada, Iceland, and Norway. This kelp is a rich source of nutrients and is free from artificial colors and preservatives.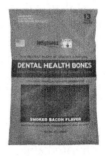

Brushing your pet's teeth is the ultimate defense for oral health. This involves the use of both a canine-specific toothbrush and toothpaste. Never use human toothpaste, which contains fluoride toxic to your dog. Some dog toothbrushes resemble smaller versions of our own, but I like the models that just fit over your fingertip. I think they offer greater control and stability.

The real trick to brushing your pet's teeth is getting the dog comfortable with having your hands in his mouth. Start by just massaging the dog's face, and then progressing to the gums before using the toothbrush. In the beginning, you can even just smear the toothpaste on the teeth with your fingertip.

Try to schedule these brushing sessions for when the dog is a little tired, perhaps after a long walk. Don't apply pressure, which can stress the dog. Just move in small circular motions and stop when the Cavachon has had enough of the whole business. If you don't feel you've done enough, stop. A second session is better than forcing your dog to do something he doesn't like and creating a negative association in his mind.

Even if you do practice a full home dental care routine, don't scrimp on annual oral exams in the vet's office. Exams not only help to keep the teeth and gums healthy, but also to check for the presence of possible cancerous growths.

TIP - If your dog will not let you brush their teeth, allow them to chew on knuckle bones, bull pizzles, cow ears or trachea. These all help remove tartar and stimulate the gums.

The Matter of Genetic Abnormalities

There is a lot of misinformation out there regarding the health of mixed breed dogs versus purebred dogs. On the surface level, it makes sense that a mixed breed dog might be less prone to inherited diseases because the gene pool is much larger than for a purebred.

In reality, however, multiple studies (and input from veterinarians) suggest that this might not be the case. The University of California-Davis conducted a five-year study on the prevalence of common inherited disorders in mixed breed and purebred dogs. According to the study, there are no differences between the two. If you talk to a veterinarian he will tell you that he sees just as many cases of hereditary conditions like hip dysplasia, progressive retina atrophy, and hypothyroidism. There is an exception to this rule, however. There are some inherited conditions which are isolated to specific breeds.

In general, the Cavachon is a very healthy breed. When it comes to health problems you can expect to see a mixture of conditions affecting the Bichon Frise and the Cavalier King Charles Spaniel.

Some of the diseases most commonly seen in Bichon Frise dogs are bladder infections, bladder stones, juvenile cataracts, diabetes mellitus, mitral valve disease, patellar luxation, and skin allergies.

Some of the most common diseases affecting the Cavalier King Charles Spaniel include brachycephalic airway obstruction syndrome, juvenile cataracts, hip dysplasia, keratoconjunctivitis, mitral valve disease and syringomyelia. As you will notice, there are a few conditions that affect both the Bichon Frise and the Cavalier King Charles Spaniel, so your Cavachon might have an increased risk for these conditions.

Health Testing the Parents

The best way to ensure that you have a healthy Cavachon is to buy from a breeder who follows responsible breeding practices. A responsible breeder will screen for inherited conditions and will not breed a dog that has hip dysplasia, epilepsy, or other conditions. This doesn't mean that your Cavachon will definitely not get one of these conditions, but it does make it much less likely.

Cavalier parents should be DNA tested for these potential issues:

- CC/DE - Curly Coat/Dry Eye (eyes produce no tears, skin very dry, coat curly and coarse).

- EF - Episodic Falling Syndrome (involuntary muscle spasms).

- Eye disease: Multifocal Retinal Dysplasia (MRD) (litter screening); Hereditary cataract (HC) (annual testing); Multiple ocular defects (MOD) (litter screening).

- Mitral Valve Disease (MVD): Both parents should be clear of heart murmur at two and a half years and grandparents clear at 5 years. MVD has a very high incidence in the breed with 50% developing heart murmurs by the age of 5 years.

- Hip Dysplasia (malformation of the hip joints causing pain and lameness).

- Chiari Malformation Syringomyelia (CMSM) (occipital bone malformation which squashes the hindbrain, blocks the normal flow of cerebrospinal fluid and causes pockets of fluid within the spinal cord) causes pain and other neurological symptoms. Most Cavaliers have the Chiari malformation and at 6 years and over 70% will have SM.

The **Bichon Frise** requires less testing but certainly the parents should be tested for eye disease: Hereditary cataract (HD) (annual testing).

The following sections give you an overview of some of the most common conditions affecting the Bichon Frise and the Cavalier King Charles Spaniel so you will be prepared in case one of these conditions affects your Cavachon.

Luxating Patella

A dog with a luxating patella experiences frequent dislocations of the kneecap. The condition is common in smaller breeds, and can affect one or both kneecaps. Surgery may be required to rectify the problem. Often, owners have no idea anything is wrong with their dog's knee joint. Then the pet jumps off a bed or leaps to catch a toy, lands badly, and begins to limp and favor the other leg.

The condition may be genetic in origin, so it is important to ask a breeder if the problem has surfaced in the line of dogs he cultivates. A luxating patella can also be the consequence of a physical injury, especially as a dog ages. For this reason, you want to **discourage jumping** in older dogs. Offer steps in key locations around the home to help your senior Cavachon navigate in safety.

Any time you see your dog limping or seeming more fatigued than usual after vigorous play, have the dog checked out. Conditions like a luxating patella only get worse with time and wear, and need immediate treatment.

Diabetes

People aren't the only ones who can get diabetes – it is also fairly common in the Bichon Frise dog breed. Diabetes occurs when the dog's pancreas can't produce enough insulin to regulate and process glucose in his diet. Diabetes most commonly develops during middle or old age and contributing factors include weight gain, inflammation, heredity, viral diseases, and certain steroidal medications.

Canines can suffer from three types of diabetes: *insipidus, diabetes mellitus,* and gestational diabetes. All point to malfunctioning endocrine glands and are often linked to poor diet. Larger dogs are in a higher risk category.

- In cases of *diabetes insipidus,* low levels of the hormone vasopressin create problems with the regulation of blood glucose, salt, and water.

- *Diabetes mellitus* is more common and dangerous. It is divided into Types I and II. The first develops in young dogs and may be referred to as 'juvenile'. Type II is more prevalent in adult and older dogs. All cases are treated with insulin.

- Gestational diabetes occurs in pregnant female dogs and requires the same treatment as diabetes mellitus. Obese dogs are at greater risk.

Abnormal insulin levels interfere with blood sugar levels. Cavachons face a high risk for diabetes if they become obese.

Symptoms of Canine Diabetes

It is possible your pet may display no symptoms whatsoever. Diabetes can be slow to develop, so the effects may not be immediately noticeable. Regular check-ups help to catch this disease, which can be fatal. All of the following behaviors are signs that a dog is suffering from canine diabetes:

- excessive water consumption
- excessive and frequent urination
- lethargy / uncharacteristic laziness

- weight gain or loss for no reason

Managing Diabetes

As part of a diabetes management program, the vet will recommend dietary changes, including special food. Your dog may need insulin injections. Although this may sound daunting, your vet will train you to administer the shots. A dog with diabetes can live a full and normal life. Expect regular visits to the vet to check for heart and circulatory problems.

Photo: Elsie from Sue Tomlin.

Heart Murmurs

These are an abnormality in the way the heartbeat sounds when listened to with a stethoscope, due to an unusual blood flow through the heart. Many Cavachons lead perfectly normal lives with this abnormality, but a heart murmur can also be an early sign of a leaking mitral valve.

With heart murmurs, although expensive, a cardiac ultrasound exam is recommended to establish the extent of a possible problem. It is also worth asking your breeder whether there has been any history of heart disease in the puppy's pedigree.

Mitral Valve Disease

This is the abnormal leaking of blood through the mitral valve, from the left ventricle into the left atrium of the heart. Over time this leak gets worse, eventually resulting in congestive heart failure.

MVD is the most common cause of death amongst Cavaliers around the world. Mitral valve disease is a genetic condition that to some degree affects approximately 50% of all Cavaliers by the age of ten (some are affected more seriously than others).

Symptoms of mitral valve disease usually progress slowly, although the speed of progression can vary. If mitral valve disease is detected, the dog should have regular checkups to monitor how the condition is progressing.

There is no cure for mitral valve disease. Drugs can often slow the deterioration of the heart valve, but these only work in the short term. The drugs used for mitral valve disease can also cause serious side effects.

Mitral valve disease is a big problem for Cavalier breeders. A recently designed protocol states that Cavaliers shouldn't be bred until they are at least five years old, which is something to keep in mind when choosing a Cavachon breeder. This is so that the breeder can be sure the Cavalier isn't going to develop MVD early in life.

Hemangiosarcoma

This is a highly aggressive malignant cancer that arises from the blood vessels, which then rapidly circulates through the bloodstream. Tumors then develop in areas such as the spleen (around 50%), and also the heart, liver, skin, kidneys, mouth, muscle, bone, brain, and bladder.

Hemangiosarcoma is called "The Silent Killer" because signs are usually not apparent until it has metastasized and the tumor has ruptured before treatment is possible. For example, it doesn't show up in blood tests until hemorrhaging has occurred, and ultrasounds fail to detect fast-growing tumors. Unfortunately, at this time the causes are unknown, but a lot of research is being done to understand the disease. Warning signs you can look out for include:

- Lethargic and cold
- Lack of appetite
- Wanting to spend time on his own
- Pale gums
- Expanded, fluid-filled abdomen (with tumors in the spleen)

Treatment is by surgery and chemotherapy, although in most cases this does not provide a cure, but it does prolong your dog's life by around six months.

Hip Dysplasia

Cavachons may also be susceptible to hip dysplasia. This defect prevents the thighbone from fitting into the hip joint. It is a painful condition that causes limping in the hindquarters. Again, this may be inherited, or the consequence of injury and aging. Limit steps until growth plates are closed at 9-12 months.

When hip dysplasia presents, the standard treatment is anti-inflammatory medication. Some cases need surgery and even a full hip replacement. Surgical intervention for this defect carries a high success rate, allowing your dog to live a **full and happy life.**

Canine Arthritis

Dogs, like humans, can suffer from arthritis, a debilitating degeneration of the joints. As the cartilage in the joints breaks down, the action of bone rubbing on bone creates considerable pain. In turn, the animal's range of motion becomes restricted.

Standard treatments do not differ from those used for humans. Aspirin addresses pain and inflammation, while supplements like glucosamine work on improving joint health. Environmental aids, like steps and ramps, ease the strain on the affected joints and help pets stay active.

Arthritis is a natural consequence of aging. Management focuses on making your pet comfortable and facilitating ease of motion. Some dogs become so crippled that their humans buy them mobility carts.

Canine Eye Care

Check your dog's eyes on a regular schedule to avoid problems like clogged tear ducts. Also, many dogs suffer from excessive tearing, which can stain the fur around the eyes and down the muzzle.

As a part of good grooming, keep the corners of your pet's eyes and the muzzle free of mucus to prevent bacterial growth. If your dog is prone to mucus accumulation, ask your vet for sterile eyewash or gauze pads. Also consider having the dog tested for environmental allergies.

With longhaired animals, take the precaution of keeping the hair well-trimmed around your pet's eyes. If you do not feel comfortable doing this chore yourself, discuss the problem with your groomer. Shorter hair prevents the transference of bacteria and avoids trauma from scrapes and scratches.

Dogs love to hang their heads out of car windows, but this can result in eye injuries and serious infection from blowing debris. If you don't want to deprive your dog of this simple pleasure, I recommend a product called Doggles. These protective goggles for dogs come in a range of colors and sizes for less than $20 / £12 per pair. The investment in protecting your dog's eyes is well worth it. All my pets have worn the Doggles without complaint.

Conjunctivitis is the **most common** eye infection seen in dogs. It presents with redness around the eyes and a green or yellow discharge. Antibiotics will treat the infection. The dreaded 'cone of shame' collar then prevents more injury from scratching during healing.

Melanie McCarthy of Cavachons From The Monarchy: "Cavachons, Bichons, Poodles and especially other non-shedding dogs are known for having excessive tearing and discharge that accumulates under the eyes; this is because non-shedding dogs do not throw off the hair under their eyes, so the tearing begins to accumulate. Non-shedding dogs should have the area around their eyes cleaned daily.

"We found a cleaner that works extremely well and if used daily, will prevent tear staining. It is '**Miracle Care Eye Care**' by 'Eye Clear'. It eliminates and prevents unsightly eye stains and is a non-stinging eye irrigation product. And of course having a 'clean' diet helps from the inside out."

Entropion

This is a condition in which the dog's eyelid turns inward, irritating the cornea. The issue becomes apparent in puppies with squinting and excessive tearing. In most cases, the condition resolves as the dog ages. In severe instances, a canine ophthalmologist must tack the lids with stitches that will remain in place for a period of days or weeks until the correct 'fit' is achieved. During healing, artificial tears are used to prevent drying of the eyes.

Distichiasis

This painful condition is caused by extra eyelashes growing from abnormal follicles on the inner surface or inside edge of the eyelid. In some cases, there is no problem if the hairs are very small, but if they are long and hard enough, they will cause irritation to the cornea. Results include corneal ulcers, chronic eye and eyelid pain, and excessive tearing.

Treatment is relatively straightforward. Both surgery or electrolysis will remove these abnormal hairs permanently by destroying the hair follicles, preventing re-growth.

Juvenile Cataracts

Juvenile cataracts is a condition known to affect both the Bichon Frise and the Cavalier King Charles Spaniel. This condition is hereditary in most cases, though it can be linked to eye trauma or diseases like diabetes mellitus.

A cataract is clouding or darkening in the lens of the eye which results from accumulated proteins. There are three types of cataracts classified by the onset of age; juvenile cataracts most commonly affect the Bichon Frise and Cavalier King Charles Spaniel.

Cataracts are very common in dogs and they may interfere with your dog's eyesight, leading to blurred vision. The lesion can vary in size and will be visible as a blue/gray area. Surgery is the only permanent solution for this problem, though many dogs adapt well to changes in vision - even total loss of vision. You should have your dog's cataracts checked by a veterinarian in any case, however, to rule out secondary complications.

In most cases, the vet will watch, but not treat, cataracts. The condition does not affect your pet's life in a severe way. Dogs adapt well to the senses they do have, so diminished vision is not as problematic as it would be for us.

Cherry Eye

The condition called 'cherry eye' is an irritation of the third eyelid. It appears as a bright pink protrusion in the corner of the eye. Cherry eye is caused by injury or a bacterial infection. It may occur in one or both eyes and requires surgery to effect a permanent cure.

Glaucoma

With glaucoma, increased pressure prevents proper drainage of fluid. Glaucoma may develop on its own, or as a complication of a shifted cataract. Dogs with glaucoma experience partial or total loss of vision within one year of diagnosis.

Symptoms include swelling, excessive tearing, redness, and evident visual limitations. Suspected glaucoma requires immediate medical attention.

Urolithiasis

The Bichon Frise is particularly prone to developing bladder infections and bladder stones. Bladder stones are called uroliths and these are an accumulation of minerals that over time have turned into crystals and stones in a dog's urinary tract.

There are several different kinds known to affect dogs; the type that most commonly affects the Bichon Frise are made from calcium oxylate. Bladder infections in Bichon Frise dogs are often linked to bacteria that produce urease, though the main cause of urolithiasis (the condition which produces uroliths) is hereditary (genetic).

Some other contributing factors for urolithiasis include poor diet or metabolic conditions like Cushing's disease.

Obvious signs are frequent urinating and accidents in the home. You may also notice him straining and showing signs of pain. You can help by making sure your Cavachon always has a supply of fresh water and making sure he doesn't have to 'hold it in' for long periods of time.

You will need to seek out veterinary help quickly before it gets serious. These blockages could prevent the passage of urine, meaning toxins in your dog's waste become trapped in his body. It may be possible to flush out the stones, but otherwise removal by surgery will be necessary.

To prevent recurrence, water consumption should be increased, the pH of the urine measured, and there are dog food manufacturers (e.g., Royal Canin, Purina) that have developed specific diets for dogs with urinary stones.

Brachycephalic Airway Obstruction Syndrome

The Cavalier King Charles Spaniel is a short-faced breed which puts it at risk for brachycephalic airway obstruction syndrome. This is not actually a single disease, but a group of upper respiratory abnormalities which include **everted laryngeal saccules, elongated soft palate, hypoplastic trachea**, and **stenotic nares**. A dog with brachycephalic airway obstruction syndrome might have one, several, or all of these conditions.

Everted laryngeal saccules involves the small pouches in the larynx getting sucked into the airway during breathing, while elongated soft palate involves the soft tissue at the roof of the dog's mouth getting pulled into the airway.

Hypoplastic trachea refers to a trachea that is too narrow, while stenotic nares are nostrils that are too small. Any of these conditions can affect the dog's breathing, causing coughing or gagging as well as reduced tolerance to exercise and heat. Some of these conditions can be managed with corticosteroids or anti-inflammatories. With hypoplastic tracheas, there is very little that can be done, however stenotic nares, elongated soft palates and everted laryngeal saccules can all be treated surgically. However, these are costly - for example soft palate resection can cost from $500 to $1,500, while stenotic nares resection varies from $200 to $1,000.

Reverse sneezing is a phenomenon of the breed that can be very startling to the Cavachon guardian when they hear this snorting, gagging or honking sound for the first time. Often it is brought on when a dog becomes overly excited from quickly eating special treats, or when greeting another dog or friend. Usually the dog will stop moving and hang its head during a reverse sneezing episode, and although it may be distressing to the dog, it is usually more distressing to the Cavachon owner.

There are several methods that can help a dog overcome a reverse sneezing episode, including calming them, rubbing their nose so that they open their mouth and begin breathing normally, and giving their chest a quick little squeeze on either side to force air out of their lungs. Sometimes, lightly blowing air into their face will also relieve the episode.

Most dogs will appear completely normal both before and after episodes of reverse sneezing and will continue to experience them intermittently throughout their lives. In severe cases, surgery is recommended, which involves applying prosthetic rings to the outside of the trachea.

Overheating can be a serious problem for dogs suffering from severe respiratory problems, because the increased panting causes further swelling and narrowing of the airways, so if your Cavachon has a severe breathing problem, it will be advisable not to exercise them in hot weather.

Keratoconjunctivitis

Also known as dry eye, keratoconjunctivitis is an eye condition known to affect the Cavalier King Charles Spaniel. This condition typically involves inflammation of the cornea and the tissues surrounding the eye. It is caused by inadequate tear production.

This condition can be caused by trauma to the eye, certain medications, hypothyroidism, systemic infection, and immune-mediated disorders that affect tear production. The most common signs of this condition include painful, red and irritated eyes: some dogs will blink excessively or keep their eyes shut. Treatment typically involves medications to stimulate tear production as well as tear film replacement in the form of eye drops.

Syringomyelia

Syringomyelia (SM) is a condition affecting the spinal cord. It can affect any dog but is more common amongst Cavaliers. The back of a Cavalier's skull is often too small for its brain, which causes a blockage in the spinal column. This prevents spinal fluid from flowing into the spinal cord, resulting in cavities at the top of the spine. The most common symptom of SM is scratching around the neck, which is often referred to as 'air scratching'.

Cavaliers also develop the condition at a younger age than other breeds. This symptom doesn't usually develop until the puppy is around six months old, which can make diagnosis difficult. As the condition develops, SM causes pain around the neck that becomes progressively worse.

SM is an extremely serious condition. There aren't many treatment options, although medication can help to manage the pain. Surgery to remove the blockage and allow spinal fluid to flow properly can sometimes stop the disease progression, but is expensive and can only be performed by specialists. The condition may start to get worse even after successful surgery, as scar tissue can form, leading to a new blockage.

Chapter 11 – Helping Your Senior Cavachon Live Longer

Obviously it can be incredibly sad to see your beloved Cavachon grow older. Unfortunately, aging is a natural part of life that cannot be avoided. All you can do is to learn how to provide for your Cavachon's needs as he ages so you can keep him with you for as long as possible.

He may develop health problems like arthritis, and he simply might not be as active as he once was. You are likely to notice a combination of both physical and mental (behavior) changes as both body and mind start to slow. With good veterinary care and proper nutrition, he can live for many more years.

Elderly Cavachons and What to Expect

Aging is a natural part of life for both humans and dogs. Sadly, dogs reach the end of their lives sooner than most humans do. Once your Cavachon reaches the age of 8 years or so, he can be considered a 'senior' dog.

At this point, you may need to start feeding him a dog food specially formulated for older dogs. Because their **metabolism slows down**, they will put on weight unless their daily calories are reduced. Unfortunately, this weight then places extra stress on their joints and organs, making them work harder than before.

Willow

Photo Credit: Linda & Steve Rogers of Timshell Farm.

In order to properly care for your Cavachon as he ages, you might find it helpful to know what to expect as your Cavachon dog starts to get older:

1. Your Cavachon's **joints** may start to give him trouble – check for signs of swelling and stiffness, often due to arthritis, and consult your veterinarian with any problems.

2. Your dog may be **less active** than he was in his youth – he will likely still enjoy walks, but he may not last as long as he once did, and he might take it at a slower pace.

3. Organs, such as heart or liver, may not function as effectively.

4. He may have an occasional 'accident' inside the house as a result of incontinence. He may also urinate more frequently.

5. Your Cavachon may **sleep more** than he once did – this is a natural sign of aging, but it can also be a symptom of a health problem, so consult your vet if your dog's sleeping becomes excessive.

6. He may have a greater tendency to **gain weight**, so you will need to carefully monitor his diet to keep him from becoming obese in his old age.

7. Brain activity is affected — your Cavachon's **memory**, ability to learn, and awareness will all start to weaken. He may wander round aimlessly or fail to respond to basic commands.

8. He may have **trouble walking** or jumping, so keep an eye on your Cavachon if he has difficulty jumping, or if he starts dragging his back feet.

9. You may need to trim your Cavachon's nails more frequently if he doesn't spend as much time outside as he once did when he was younger.

10. Your Cavachon will develop gray hair around the face and muzzle – this may be less noticeable in Cavachons with a lighter coat.

11. Your Cavachon's **vision** may deteriorate. Be careful if his eyes appear cloudy. This could be a sign of cataracts and you should see your vet as soon as you notice this.

12. He may develop halitosis (bad breath), which can be a sign of dental or gum disease. Get this checked out by a vet. Brush his teeth to a regular schedule.

While many of the signs mentioned above are natural side effects of aging, they can also be symptoms of serious health conditions. If your Cavachon develops any of these problems suddenly, consult your veterinarian immediately.

Tips for Caring for Dogs in Old Age

When your Cavachon gets older, he may require different care than he did when he was younger. The more you know about what to expect as your Cavachon ages, the better equipped you will be to provide him with the care he needs to remain healthy and mobile.

1. Supplement your dog's diet with DHA and EPA fatty acids to help prevent joint stiffness and arthritis.

2. Schedule routine annual visits with your veterinarian to make sure your Cavachon is in good condition.

3. He may be more sensitive to extreme heat and cold, so make sure he has a comfortable place to lie down both inside and outside.

4. Consider switching to a dog food that is specially formulated for senior/mature dogs – a food that is too high in calories may cause your dog to gain weight. Some are labeled as from age 8, others for even older dogs such as 10+. Take it slow when switching to minimize the impact on their digestive system, which cannot cope with sudden change.

5. Brush your Cavachon's teeth regularly to prevent

periodontal diseases, which are fairly common in older dogs. A daily dental stick helps reduce tartar, freshen breath and improve gum health.

6. Continue to exercise your dog on a regular basis – he may not be able to move as quickly, but you still need to keep him active to maintain joints, muscle health and vital organs such as heart, lungs and joints.

7. Provide your Cavachon with **soft bedding** on which to sleep – the hard floor may aggravate his joints and worsen arthritis.

8. Ensure his usual environment is not too noisy, as he will need to rest and sleep more to recharge his body. Make sure it is neither too hot nor cold, as his body may not regulate his temperature as well as he used to.

9. Consider putting down carpet or rugs on hard floors – slippery hardwood or tile flooring can be very problematic for arthritic dogs.

10. Keep your Cavachon's **mind exercised** as well as his body. Playing games and introducing new toys will achieve this.

11. Use **ramps** to get your dog into the car and onto the bed (if he is allowed), because he may no longer be able to jump.

When Cavachons become elderly they are likely to exhibit certain changes in behavior, including:

• Confusion or disorientation
• Increased irritability
• Decreased responsiveness to commands
• Increase in vocalization (barking, whining, etc.)
• Heightened reaction to sound
• Increased aggression or protectiveness
• Changes in sleep habits
• Increase in house soiling accidents

As he ages, these tendencies may increase – he may also become more protective of you around strangers.

As your Cavachon gets older, you may find that he responds to your commands even **less frequently** than he used to.

The most important thing you can do for your senior dog is to schedule regular visits with your veterinarian. You should also, however, keep an eye out for signs of disease as your dog ages.

The following are common signs of disease in elderly dogs:

• Decreased appetite
• Increased thirst and urination
• Difficulty urinating/constipation
• Blood in the urine
• Difficulty breathing/coughing
• Vomiting or diarrhea
• Poor coat condition

If you notice your elderly Cavachon exhibiting any of these symptoms, you would be wise to seek veterinary care for your dog as soon as possible.

Why I Recommend Pet Insurance

I believe in preventive maintenance as much as possible. My own dogs are seen by a veterinary chiropractor fairly regularly from the time they are about 9 weeks old, and they are well exercised to avoid the 'weekend athlete' injuries. I have been blessed with overall sound and healthy Cavachons but nevertheless I wouldn't be without my pet health insurance just in case the worst happens.

Thanks to advances in veterinary science, our pets now receive viable and effective treatments. The estimated annual cost for a medium-sized dog, including health care, is $650 / £387. (This does not include emergency care, advanced procedures, or consultations with specialists.)

The growing interest in pet insurance to help defray these costs is understandable. You can buy a policy covering accidents, illness, and hereditary and chronic conditions for $25 / £16.25 per month. Benefit caps and deductibles vary by company.

Although breeders are now becoming more responsible in improving the overall health of a breed, it is inevitable that you will need to make a number of visits to the vets in your Cavachon's lifetime. Apart from the routine of annual injections and check-ups, there are bound to be unexpected visits, often at weekends or in the middle of the night when costs are significantly higher. This total can run to thousands of dollars (or pounds).

Establishing a healthy record from the very beginning ensures your Cavachon qualifies for full insurance coverage and lower premiums.

To get rate quotes, investigate the following companies in the United States and the UK:

United States of America

http://www.24PetWatch.com
http://www.ASPCAPetInsurance.com
http://www.PetsBest.com
http://www.PetInsurance.com

United Kingdom

http://www.Animalfriends.org.uk
http://www.Healthy-pets.co.uk
http://www.Petplan.co.uk

Grieving a Lost Pet

The hardest decision any pet owner makes is helping a suffering animal to pass easily and humanely. I have been in this position. Even though I know my beloved companions died peacefully and with no pain, my own anguish was considerable. Thankfully, I was in the care of and accepting the advice and counsel of exceptional veterinary professionals.

This is the crucial component in the decision to euthanize an animal. For your own peace of mind, you must know that you have the best medical advice possible. My vet was not only knowledgeable and patient, but she was kind and forthright. I valued those qualities and hope you are as blessed as I was in the same situation.

The bottom line is that you must make the best decision that you can for your pet, and for yourself. So long as you are acting from a position of love, respect, and responsibility, whatever you do is 'right'.

Photo Credit: Jan Stocks.

Some humans have difficulty fully recognizing the terrible grief involved in losing a beloved canine friend. There will be many who **do not understand** the close bond we humans can have with our dogs, which is often unlike any we have with our human counterparts.

Your friends may give you pitying looks and try to cheer you up, but if they have never experienced the loss of such a special connection themselves, they may also secretly think you are making too much fuss over 'just a dog'.

For some of us humans, the loss of a beloved dog is so painful that we decide never to share our lives with another, because the thought of going through the pain of such a loss is unbearable.

Expect to feel terribly sad, tearful, and yes, depressed, because those who are close to their canine companions will feel their loss no less acutely than the loss of a human friend or life partner. The grieving process can take some time to recover from, and some of us never totally recover.

After the loss of a family dog, first you need to take care of yourself by making certain that you remember to eat regular meals and get enough sleep, even though you will feel an almost eerie sense of loneliness.

Losing a beloved dog is a shock to the system that can also affect your concentration and your ability to find joy or be interested in participating in other activities that are a normal part of your daily life.

Other dogs, cats, and pets in the home will also be grieving the loss of a companion and may display this by acting depressed, being off their food, or showing little interest in play or games. Therefore, you need to help guide your other pets through this grieving process by keeping them busy and interested, taking them for extra walks, and finding ways to spend more time with them.

Wait Long Enough

Many people **do not wait long enough** before attempting to replace a lost pet and will immediately go to the local shelter and rescue a deserving dog. While this may help to distract you from your grieving process, this is not really fair to the new fur member of your family.

Bringing a new pet into a home that is depressed and grieving the loss of a long-time canine member may create behavioral problems for the new dog that will be faced with learning all about their new home, while also dealing with the unstable energy of the grieving family.

A better scenario would be to **allow yourself the time to properly grieve** by waiting a minimum of one month to give yourself and your family time to feel happier and more stable before deciding upon sharing your home with another dog.

Afterword

With so many different dog breeds to choose from, picking just one can be difficult. Ultimately, picking a dog breed comes down to determining which characteristics you like most in a dog. If you want a dog that is friendly, social, and great with kids, then the Cavachon might be the dog for you.

I have no doubt that a Cavachon will live up to your every expectation of what a perfect dog should be - just make sure you can be the perfect human for him!

Cavachons are unique in that they possess a combination of traits from the Bichon Frise and the Cavalier King Charles Spaniel. These dogs are fun-loving and people-oriented which makes them excellent family pets and companions. Once your Cavachon bonds with you, you will have a best friend for life.

Photo Credit: Nichola Lack of Cracking Cavachons.

Glossary

Abdomen – The surface area of a dog's body lying between the chest and the hindquarters, also referred to as the belly.

Allergy – An abnormally sensitive reaction to substances including pollens, foods, or microorganisms. May be present in humans or animals with similar symptoms including, but not limited to, sneezing, itching, and skin rashes.

Anal glands – Glands located on either side of a dog's anus, used to mark territory. May become blocked and require treatment by a veterinarian.

Arm – On a dog, the region between the shoulder and the elbow is referred to as the arm or the upper arm.

Back – That portion of a dog's body that extends from the withers (or shoulder) to the croup (approximately the area where the back flows into the tail.)

Bitch – The appropriate term for a female dog.

Blooded – An accepted reference to a pedigreed dog.

Breed – A line or race of dogs selected and cultivated by man from a common gene pool to achieve and maintain a characteristic appearance and function.

Breed standard – A written 'picture' of a perfect specimen of a given breed in terms of appearance, movement, and behavior as formulated by a parent organization, for example, the American Kennel Club or in Great Britain, The Kennel Club.

Brows – The contours of the frontal bone that form ridges above a dog's eyes.

Buttocks – The hips or rump of a dog.

Castrate – The process of removing a male dog's testicles.

Chest – That portion of a dog's trunk or body encased by the ribs.

Coat – The hair covering a dog. Most breeds have both an outer coat and an undercoat.

Come into Season – The point at which a female dog becomes fertile for purposes of mating.

Congenital – Any quality, particularly an abnormality, present at birth.

Crate – Any portable container used to house a dog for transport or provided to a dog in the home as a 'den'.

Crossbred – Dogs are said to be crossbred when each of their parents is of a different breed.

Dam – A term for the female parent.

Dew Claw – The dew claw is an extra claw on the inside of the leg. It is a rudimentary fifth toe.

Euthanize – The act of relieving the suffering of a terminally ill animal by inducing a humane death, typically with an overdose of anesthesia.

Fancier – Any person with an exceptional interest in purebred dogs and the shows where they are exhibited.

Groom – To make a dog's coat neat by brushing, combing, or trimming.

Harness - A cloth or leather strap shaped to fit the shoulders and chest of a dog with a ring at the top for attaching a lead. An alternative to using a collar.

Haunch Bones – Terminology for the hip bones of a dog.

Haw – The membrane inside the corner of a dog's eye, known as the third eyelid.

Head – The cranium and muzzle of a dog.

Hip Dysplasia – A condition in dogs due to a malformation of the hip, resulting in painful and limited movement of varying degrees.

Hindquarters – The back portion of a dog's body including the pelvis, thighs, hocks, and paws.

Hock – Bones on the hind leg of a dog that form the joint between the second thigh and the metatarsus. Known as the dog's true heel.

Lead – Any strap, cord, or chain used to restrain or lead a dog. Typically attached to a collar or harness. Also called a leash.

Litter – The puppy or puppies from a single birth or 'whelping'.

Muzzle – The portion of a dog's head lying in front of the eyes and consisting of the nasal bone, nostrils, and jaws.

Neuter – To castrate or spay a dog thus rendering them incapable of reproducing.

Pedigree – The written record of a pedigreed dog's genealogy. Should extend to three or more generations.

Puppy – Any dog of less than 12 months of age.

Separation Anxiety – The anxiety and stress suffered by a dog left alone for any period of time.

Sire – The accepted term for the male parent.

Spay – The surgery to remove a female dog's ovaries to prevent conception.

Whelping – Term for the act of giving birth to puppies.

Withers – The highest point of a dog's shoulders.